Representations of Transnational Human Trafficking

Christiana Gregoriou
Editor

Representations of Transnational Human Trafficking

Present-day News Media, True Crime, and Fiction

Editor
Christiana Gregoriou
School of English
University of Leeds
Leeds, UK

ISBN 978-3-319-78213-3   ISBN 978-3-319-78214-0   (eBook)
https://doi.org/10.1007/978-3-319-78214-0

Library of Congress Control Number: 2018945918

Cover pattern © Harvey Loake

Printed on acid-free paper

This Palgrave Pivot imprint is published by the registered company Springer International
Publishing AG part of Springer Nature.
The registered company address is: Gewerbestrasse 11, 6330 Cham, Switzerland

EDITOR'S PREFACE, ACKNOWLEDGMENTS AND RECOMMENDATIONS

In September 2017, we convened a group of human trafficking specialist academics, police officers, third sector, Home Office and media reps, creative writers, and filmmakers to discuss findings from the AHRC and ESRC-funded 'Media Human Trafficking Representation' project (under the Partnership for Conflict, Crime and Security Research), findings this book showcases in detail. We take this opportunity to thank our invited speakers: the Police and Crime Commissioner and Chair of the National Anti-Trafficking and Modern Day Slavery Network Mark Burns-Williamson, journalist/writer/filmmaker Paul Kenyon, crime writer Matt Johnson, academic/writer/'Free the Slaves' Foundation founder Professor Kevin Bales (University of Nottingham) and academic/filmmaker Professor Nicola Mai (Kingston University), whose film *Travel*, featuring and produced alongside trafficked women, was screened. Our symposium also featured a talk by project partner Special Policing Consultant Bernie Gravett, who offered comments on the extent to which the described popular media portrayals reflect the realities of trafficking. The input and subsequent discussion highlighted the subject's complexity and brought to light several controversial issues, including media distortions shaped by economic forces that compel creative producers to turn human trafficking accounts into 'newsworthy' stories, and the challenge of communicating these stories in translation. We also identified trends and practices that generate stereotypes, clichés, and reductively formulaic human trafficking narratives. At the same time, documentaries offer powerful and affective representations, while language has the power not just to manipulate but also open up and enable deep understandings.

Given the need for stronger and more effective press regulation, we propose instituting human-trafficking-specific guidance documents, and/ or a code of practice for all who report on the issue, who need to fully appreciate the term's legal meaning and relevant ideological implications of their linguistic choices, and avoid seeing stories as mere commodities/ entertainment and as areas where truth can be manipulated. Seeking the support of those who can influence the discussion on media accuracy and encourage responsible reporting is key. We propose developing research-led material that can be used for online or in-person training/workshops for relevant practitioners in all fields (including police officers, media representatives, educationalists, and film/soap script writers), but also A-level and university students. We would also recommend generating research-led media footage or actively contributing to mainstream audience films that more accurately and sensitively report on the issue, and seek out to do briefings for various committees, foundations, and even airport/airline staff, helping identify concerning situations/individuals, improving relevant information posters (say, at airports), and ultimately informing better policy development. Lastly, there is a need to encourage and enable victims to represent themselves, in their own words/forums, devolving power down from the conventional editor/journalist decision- and programme-makers. Third-sector representatives, but also migrant rights and sex worker rights organisations, with sensitivity and access to such victims, could help them collaborate with researchers in gaining that power.

Leeds, UK   Christiana Gregoriou

CONTENTS

NOTES ON CONTRIBUTORS

Charlotte Beyer is a Senior Lecturer in English Studies at the University of Gloucestershire. Her forthcoming crime fiction publications include editing *Teaching Crime Fiction* for Palgrave, and a monograph on the crime short story (McFarland). She is also co-editing three Demeter Press books, *Mothers Without Their Children* with Andrea Robertson; *Travellin' Mama: Mothers, Mothering and Travel* with Janet MacLennan, Dorsía Smith Silva, and Marjorie Tesser, and *Mothers Who Kill/ Infanticide* with Josephine Savarese. Charlotte is on the Steering Committee for the Crime Studies Network and on the Editorial Boards for *Feminist Encounters, The New Americanist,* and *American, British and Canadian Studies.*

Melissa Dearey is a Senior Lecturer in Criminology in the School of Social Sciences and Faculty of Arts, Cultures and Education at the University of Hull in the UK. Her academic background is in philosophy and cultural theory, focusing on the link between politics, art/aesthetics, deviance and social change. She has published research on a broad number of topics including radicalisation, political imprisonment, diabolical evil and the moving, somatic body. She is especially interested in interdisciplinary and cultural criminology, and has adapted methodologies and concepts from dance, and popular cultural forms like auto/biography, true crime, reality TV, and game shows into her research. She is also interested in green criminology, that is, corporate and state crimes against nature and non-human animals.

Christiana Gregoriou is an Associate Professor in English Language at Leeds University. She is a crime fiction stylistics specialist and ran the 2016–2017 AHRC/ESRC-funded project on the representation of transnational human trafficking in news media, true crime, and fiction. Most notable are her three monographs (*Crime Fiction Migration: Crossing Languages, Cultures, Media*, 2017; *Language, Ideology and Identity in Serial Killer Narratives*, 2011; *Deviance in Contemporary Crime Fiction*, 2007), and her edited collections (*Constructing Crime: Discourse and Cultural Representations of Crime and 'Deviance'*, 2012; *Language and Literature*, 'Investigating Contemporary Crime Writing' special edition 21(3), 2012).

Nina Muždeka is an Associate Professor of Anglophone literatures at the University of Novi Sad, in Serbia. Her areas of interest include contemporary literature in English with a special focus on theory of genre, narratology, postmodern theory, and translation theory. She is the author of monographs on the issue of genre in Julian Barnes's novels (2006) and magical realism in Angela Carter's novels (2016). She is currently preparing a monograph on twentieth-century British detective fiction written by women. As a literary translator, Nina has translated and published over 35 full-length books of mostly contemporary Anglophone fiction.

Ilse A. Ras completed her PhD in English Language at the University of Leeds. She also holds an MSc in Criminology from the University of Leicester and is a co-founder of the Poetics and Linguistics Association Special Interest Group on Crime Writing. Her work and teaching often crosses the boundaries between English language and Criminology, focusing on the use of language to express, maintain, and reinforce (capitalist) power structures, using corpus-assisted critical discourse analysis and critical stylistics to examine this language.

LIST OF TABLES

CHAPTER 1

Representations of Transnational Human Trafficking: A Critical Review

Christiana Gregoriou and Ilse A. Ras

Abstract The collection introduction defines human trafficking and proceeds to offer an in-depth literature review that assesses the significance of attention to the collection topic, suggests new directions for research, and provides a synopsis and integrative analysis of the collective contributions of manuscripts within the collection. It starts by detailing the story of human trafficking (the types, causes, and frames of trafficking), then discusses the effects of misrepresentation on the directly affected (draws on victim hierarchy, criminalisation and secondary victimisation), and then deals with the socio-political causes and effects of misrepresentation (gender and wealth inequality, global and local politics, and secondary exploitation). It ends by providing a rationale as to the nature of the case studies the book and its contributors consider.

Keywords Criminalisation • Human trafficking • (Mis)representation • Transnational organised crime • Victim hierarchy

C. Gregoriou (✉) • I. A. Ras
School of English, University of Leeds, Leeds, UK
e-mail: c.gregoriou@leeds.ac.uk; i.a.ras@leeds.ac.uk

© The Author(s) 2018
C. Gregoriou (ed.), *Representations of Transnational Human Trafficking*, https://doi.org/10.1007/978-3-319-78214-0_1

1

INTRODUCTION

This collection's various studies examine representations of human trafficking (henceforth HT), traffickers, and victims in media ranging from British and Serbian newspapers, British and Scandinavian crime novels, and a documentary series, before questioning the extent to which these portrayals actually reflect the realities of trafficking. We show that media reporting on HT matters, and is impactful; HT victims are idealised, with those not according to this ideal being criminalised. Selected official source aspects of HT take priority over others that are neglected, and hence frame HT in problematic ways. Instead, fictional and factional representations of this crime can be better used as tools with which change in HT victim treatment can be engendered. Our studies focus on news articles, crime fiction, and documentaries published and released post-2000, the year in which the UN Office on Drugs and Crime Protocol to the Convention on Transnational Organised Crime, on trafficking (nicknamed the Palermo Protocol), was passed, and covers a time period in which the Modern Slavery Act 2015 was passed and the refugee and migrant crisis spread across Europe. Whilst we primarily focus on British news, fiction, and documentaries, we have also included Scandinavian crime fiction and Serbian news to facilitate comparisons with, respectively, a literary tradition that focuses on social realist themes (Brunsdale, 2016), and news from a country affected by trafficking in three dimensions (origin, transfer, and destination) and on the route of refugees from Syria, Afghanistan, and Iraq (European Commission, 2017).

We adopt the definition of trafficking set out in the Anti-Slavery International RACE Project report on 'Trafficking for Forced Criminal Activities and Begging in Europe' (2014, p. 86):

> Trafficking involves bringing people away from the communities in which they live and forcing them into work against their will using violence, deception or coercion. When children are trafficked, no violence, deception or coercion needs to be involved: simply transporting them into exploitative conditions constitutes trafficking.

This definition follows the UN (Palermo) Protocol to Prevent, Suppress and Punish Trafficking in Persons Especially Women and Children, supplementing the United Nations Convention against Transnational Organized Crime (UNODC, 2016, passed in 2000). We acknowledge that this definition is problematic, as its terms are difficult to define, and it is difficult to establish where the thresholds of the lack of consent, and the level of deception, exploitation, coercion, and movement are located.

Previous research on the representations of HT shows that these narratives are often overly focused on only one form of HT and one particular type of victim, with the highly damaging effect of ignoring or even criminalising (other) victims of other types of HT. As such, we are critical of representations that serve to limit those forms of exploitation, force, deception, or movement, that are considered 'proper' forms of HT, and that serve to distinguish between 'real' and 'unreal' victims of HT. We argue that the characteristics of the HT narrative sustain the global structures that make people vulnerable to being trafficked in the first place. These include gender and wealth inequality, and the geopolitical power balance that primarily benefits the global West.

This introductory chapter first examines the commonly accepted definitions and narratives of HT, as found in previous studies. It then traces the effects of these stories on those vulnerable people who are trafficked, or smuggled and exploited at their destinations. Finally, it considers the global inequalities that are perpetuated by these narratives, before this collection's chapters are outlined.

THE STORY AND TRUTH(S) OF HUMAN TRAFFICKING

Media representations inform public and practitioners as to the nature of HT: they are seen and referenced by policymakers and therefore shape discourse on HT (Small, 2012). The increasing 'celebritisation' of the problem, with the rise of celebrity activists as rescuers, 'ambassadors', and (often ill-informed) 'experts', also signals pop culture's powerful role in anti-trafficking movements (Haynes, 2014, cited in Kinney, 2015, p. 90; see also Steele, 2015). Wylie (2016) traces the rise of a particular version of the story of human trafficking, and its adoption into 'common knowledge', drawing on the concept of the norm lifecycle in International Relations (Finnemore & Sikkink, 1998, in Wylie, 2016). In this lifecycle, a norm is first campaigned for by moral entrepreneurs, then supported by global actors (ibid.). If enough global actors support the new norm, others are pushed to accept it also (ibid.). The norm is then enacted on local levels, and finally becomes 'common knowledge' (ibid.). Wylie (2016) points out that the norm only successfully completes this lifecycle if it is in line with pre-existing norms, and can be used to support the material and immaterial interests of global and local actors.

Wylie (2016, p. 2) notes that in the past 20 years, a particular version of the human trafficking story has become the new normal. Winterdyk, Reichel, and Perrin (2012, p. 9) indicate that the first decade of the twenty-first century met with 'an explosion of media coverage' of HT, which they partially attribute to the passing of the Palermo Protocol in 2000. Wylie (2016) instead identifies the Palermo Protocol as part of the lifecycle. This increase in reporting would, initially, appear to be a positive development, as the public's and (untrained) practitioners' understanding of what HT is, and who the victims are, is dependent on media representations (De Shalit, Heynen, & Van der Meulen, 2014; Denton, 2010; Farrell & Fahy, 2009; Papadouka, Evangelopoulos, & Ignatow, 2016; Sanford, Martínez, & Weitzer, 2016; Sobel, 2016). Problematically, however, the 'master' narrative of HT (Snajdr, 2013; see also Wilson & O'Brien, 2016), or the version of the story of human trafficking that has become the new normal (Wylie, 2016), is full of, and based on, unreliable statistics, maps, and visual images, and selective, binary, and simplified representations (ibid.). The RACE Project report suggests that most HT cases go unreported in the media, but even when they are reported, they are often devoid of details such as nationality, age, outcome/sentence length of those convicted, and indicators of trafficking (e.g., confinement, passport loss, and no or minimal pay).

Simplification

The difficulty in representing HT accurately is illustrated by the misuse of labels such as 'trafficking' and 'smuggling'. Legally, the former is a crime against an individual and can be intranational, while the latter is a crime against the state and is, necessarily, transnational. Unlike trafficking, smuggling is presumed to be consensual on the part of the smuggled (Lobasz, 2009, p. 328). The reality of trafficking/smuggling is not quite so clear. '[S]ome argue that human trafficking and migrant smuggling are better thought of as two ends of a continuum' (Lobasz, 2009, p. 328), the concepts being 'intricately intertwined' (Aronowitz, 2009, p. 4). Consent may be blurry or absent at various stages of either process. Both those trafficked and those smuggled are susceptible to exploitation (O'Connell Davidson, 2010, p. 249; Piper, Segrave, & Napier-Moore, 2015). Those who have been smuggled and are exploited later are, legally, victims of trafficking, even if, at the border, they are considered as having been smuggled (Kara, 2010, p. 189; Lobasz, 2009, p. 328; Wylie, 2016, p. 6).

Kelly (2005) indicates that the length of the journey increases the probability that a person is coerced or deceived, as well as exploited, as longer journeys increase people's vulnerability. Exploitation may also be done by people other than the smugglers, due to the undocumented status of those smuggled (Wylie, 2016, p. 6). This interconnection might explain why the media and the public tend to conflate the two (Dando, Walsh, & Brierley, 2016; Denton, 2010; Farrell & Fahy, 2009; Marchionni, 2012; Papadouka et al., 2016; Winterdyk et al., 2012).

The problem does not just lie with the media conflating the two concepts, but with how the distinction is made. Male irregular migrants are generally presumed smuggled, thus presumed as having consented to their movement, whereas female irregular migrants are generally presumed trafficked, as not having consented to movement (De Shalit et al., 2014; Musto, 2009). As a result, the (male) smuggled migrant is criminalised, whilst the (female) trafficked migrant is assigned victim-status (Hua & Nigorizawa, 2010, pp. 406–407). The differentiation between trafficked and smuggled migrant may also depend on whether they are perceived as having been 'exploited enough', creating a distinction between 'deserving' and 'undeserving' migrants (Wylie, 2016, p. 6). This distinction also distracts from the fact that both smuggled and trafficked people are often vulnerable, escaping a local environment plagued by poverty, conflict, disaster, or all of the above, searching, despite the many risks involved, for a better place in which to live and work.

Types of Trafficking

The Palermo Protocol refers to all forms of labour as potential forms of exploitation (De Shalit et al., 2014, p. 392), even though it privileges sex trafficking (Wylie, 2016). Throughout media representations, the focus tends to be on sex trafficking (Alvarez & Alessi, 2012; Buckley, 2009; Denton, 2010; Dijk, 2013; Farrell & Fahy, 2009; Kelly, 2005; Lobasz, 2009; Marchionni, 2012; Moore & Goldberg, 2015; Papadouka et al., 2016; Segrave, 2009; Wylie, 2016; Yick, 2010), an assessment statistically supported by Marchionni's (2012) classification of the types of trafficking normally reported:

- Sex: 51.5%
- Labour: 4.1%
- Domestic: 2.3%

- Other: 9.4%
- Several: 4.9%
- Non-specific: 27.8%

Academic work on trafficking is similarly skewed toward analyses of discourses on the sexual exploitation of women (Duong, 2014), a focus that Szörényi and Eate (2014) attribute to sex trafficking being easily sensationalised. Lobasz (2009) similarly claims that sex trafficking is a 'sexy' topic. This focus on sex is particularly problematic when it results in the underrepresentation of other forms of HT.

In reality, most victims are trafficked for labour exploitation (O'Brien, 2016, p. 210; Feingold, 2005), and HT mainly exists in highly labour-intensive, insecure industries, such as agriculture and the gig-economy (Alvarez & Alessi, 2012; Coghlan & Wylie, 2011; Kara, 2010; Kelly, 2005; O'Brien, 2016). Trafficking for domestic services also receives little attention. Given its domestic nature, it is difficult to estimate how much such trafficking actually takes place (Kelly, 2005). Other underreported forms of trafficking include fraudulent marriages, illegal adoption, and pregnancy surrogacy (Duong, 2014).

Victims and Traffickers

The stereotypical global victim of trafficking is '[a] young, naïve woman who seeks a better life away from her rural home by answering an advertisement to become a waitress or a nanny and then ends up a sex slave, repeatedly raped, brutalised, and resold to other mafia pimps' (Lobasz, 2009, p. 340): she is *female* (Alvarez & Alessi, 2012; Andrijasevic & Mai, 2016; Columb, 2015; De Shalit et al., 2014; de Villiers, 2016; Dijk, 2013; Duong, 2014; Farrell & Fahy, 2009; Hall, 2015; Johnston, Friedman, & Sobel, 2015; Lobasz, 2009; O'Brien, 2016; Pajnik, 2010; Plambech, 2016; Russell, 2014; Sanchez, 2016; Sanford et al., 2016; Sharma, 2005; Small, 2012; Sobel, 2016; Szörényi & Eate, 2014; Wilson & O'Brien, 2016; Yick, 2010), *young* (Andrijasevic & Mai, 2016; de Villiers, 2016; Dijk, 2013; Farrell & Fahy, 2009; Hall, 2015; Hua & Nigorizawa, 2010; Johnston et al., 2015; Kara, 2010; Lobasz, 2009; O'Brien, 2016; Sanchez, 2016; Sanford et al., 2016; Small, 2012; Szörényi & Eate, 2014; Wilson & O'Brien, 2016; Yick, 2010), and *unwilling to perform the work she is doing, but coerced* (Andrijasevic & Mai, 2016; Farrell & Fahy, 2009; Lobasz, 2009; O'Brien, 2016; Sanchez, 2016). Alternatively, children may be identified as victims (Alvarez & Alessi, 2012; Johnston et al., 2015; Plambech, 2016; Sanford et al., 2016; Sharma, 2005; Sobel, 2014; Wilson & O'Brien, 2016); they too are portrayed as weak/vulnerable, and generally presumed blameless/trafficked against their will. Further to being common in news media and pop culture, these stereotypes are also shared by policy makers and the public (Buckley, 2009; Dando et al., 2016; Gould, 2010; Musto, 2009). Even more so, these characteristics are also consistent with Christie's (1986) 'ideal victim'.

One can argue that the focus on women and children as victims reflects reality; official figures do indicate that it is women and children that are most often labelled as trafficked, presumably due to the focus on sex trafficking (Cunningham & DeMarni Cromer, 2016; Dijk, 2013; Duong, 2014; Marchionni, 2012, Musto, 2009). Males, more often trafficked for labour exploitation, tend to be considered as having been 'smuggled', rather than 'trafficked', and tend to be classified as (illegal) labour migrants, rather than as victims of HT (Lobasz, 2009, p. 339). Wylie (2016, p. 5) similarly points out that many different people and institutions contribute to these figures, and each contribution is filtered through idiosyncratic understandings of what trafficking is, and who can be trafficked. Either way, men are seldom considered as victims, meaning that male victims are generally overlooked (Alvarez & Alessi, 2012; Duong, 2014; Sharma, 2005). In fact, under Thai law, it has been assumed that men cannot be victims of trafficking (Feingold, 2005).

The trafficker, in the meanwhile, is painted as 'big and bad', a shadowy, mysterious, powerful figure, often male (De Shalit et al., 2014; de Villiers, 2016; Hua & Nigorizawa, 2010; Lobasz, 2009; Moore & Goldberg, 2015; O'Brien, 2016; Pajnik, 2010; Plambech, 2016; Sanford et al., 2016; Sobel, 2016; Wilson & O'Brien, 2016; Yick, 2010), with generally no mention of whether the victim and trafficker had any prior relation. The offender is simply established as the polar opposite of the victim (Szörényi & Eate, 2014), even though in reality, this distinction may be unclear. There are indicators that a substantial number of traffickers have previously been trafficked (De Shalit et al., 2014; Moore & Goldberg, 2015). Lastly, 'johns', or the consumers of sex work, are only occasionally mentioned (O'Brien, 2016; Sobel, 2016), only occasionally held responsible for sex trafficking, and are generally identified as male (Kara, 2010; Moore & Goldberg, 2015; Sanchez, 2016).

Causes of Trafficking

In media reporting and legislation, structural causes that leave people vulnerable to being trafficked as well as smuggled are systematically ignored (Coghlan & Wylie, 2011; Johnston et al., 2015; O'Brien, 2016; Piper et al., 2015; Sanford et al., 2016; Sharma, 2005; Steele, 2015; Szörényi & Eate, 2014; Weitzer, 2007; Wilson & O'Brien, 2016). Wilson and O'Brien (2016, pp. 33, 40) argue that the US Annual Trafficking in Persons Report reinforces 'the representation of human trafficking as a criminal justice issue, constructing victims as passive agents of the criminal behaviour of offenders', 'as opposed to [treating HT as] an economic and political human rights issue'. Officials prefer to focus on the individuals that are directly involved than on structural causes (see also Wylie, 2016).

Structural push factors include *local poverty* (Duong, 2014; Farrell & Fahy, 2009; Feingold, 2005; Howard, 2012; Kara, 2010; Kelly, 2005; Moore & Goldberg, 2015; Sharma, 2005; Sobel, 2014), *gender and economic inequality* (Avendaño & Fanning, 2013; Columb, 2015; Farrell & Fahy, 2009; Hoefinger, 2016; Howard, 2012; Hua & Nigorizawa, 2010; Kara, 2010; Kelly, 2005; Moore & Goldberg, 2015; Sobel, 2014), *globalisation* (Avendaño & Fanning, 2013; Hoefinger, 2016; Segrave, 2009; Sharma, 2005), *conflicts and violence* (Feingold, 2005; Kelly, 2005; Limoncelli, 2009; Sharma, 2005) and *the difficulty in obtaining work permits*, which leaves migrant workers vulnerable to exploitation (Limoncelli, 2009; Moore & Goldberg, 2015).

Similarly, there is little attention, in both the media and legislation, to pull factors, including *the global demand for cheap labour* (Avendaño & Fanning, 2013; Duong, 2014; Feingold, 2005; Kelly, 2005; Kara, 2010; Limoncelli, 2009; O'Brien, 2016; Segrave, 2009; Sharma, 2005) and *cheap sex* (Kara, 2010; Limoncelli, 2009; Moore & Goldberg, 2015; Russell, 2014; Segrave, 2009; Sharma, 2005). Even in academic research on trafficking, 'demand' is often only addressed almost incidentally, with a few notable exceptions (see Kara, 2010).

Framing

The reasons given as to why HT must be addressed change in line with changing political priorities. Farrell and Fahy (2009) show that historically, at least in the USA, HT was framed as a woman's rights issue, ostensibly aiming to protect women, though more likely aiming to keep women docile and at home. More recently, HT has been re-framed as a criminal issue, with the result that the USA has passed various laws aimed at criminalising traffickers (and indeed some victims). Post-9/11, the issue has been re-framed again, now as a matter of national security. US policies changed correspondingly, aiming to secure borders, thereby actually increasing the vulnerability of both victims of trafficking and irregular migrants. Marchionni (2012) found that in Britain, HT has become part of discourses about policing and border control.

As Hua and Nigorizawa (2010, p. 402) put it, official discourses on trafficking

> create a dominant narrative of victimization that helps define who is 'genuinely' trafficked (and who is not). These dominant narratives rely on and reproduce troubling gender–race–nation discourses of victimization, which construct a stereotype of the 'helpless victim' that links femininity to dependency and racial 'otherness' to cultural deviancy.

In general, victims are portrayed as helpless and trapped. Meanwhile, nation states and state-sanctioned (male) actors responding to threats within their borders are set up as 'saviours' (De Shalit et al., 2014; de Villiers, 2016; Hill, 2016; Hua & Nigorizawa, 2010; Krsmanovic, 2016; O'Brien, 2016; Pajnik, 2010; Russell, 2014; Szörényi & Eate, 2014; Van der Pijl, Oude Breuil, & Siegel, 2011).

The effect of this dominant narrative is not just that the sex trafficking of young females is prioritised above all others, although that is in itself an issue. More problematically, it harms those victims who do not conform to these stereotypes.

EFFECTS OF MISREPRESENTATION ON THE DIRECTLY AFFECTED

The misrepresentation of HT means that many cases of trafficking are not recognised as such by the public (see Dando et al., 2016). The prioritisation of sex trafficking means that issues such as labour exploitation are pushed to the background (Duong, 2014; Farrell & Fahy, 2009; Lobasz, 2009; Mendel & Sharapov, 2016, p. 674; Wilson & O'Brien, 2016, p. 41), both in terms of media attention and in terms of policy. Even more concerningly, the representation of victims creates a victim hierarchy, resulting in many non-ideal, but real, victims being denied services and rights, to the extent where they are prosecuted (Alvarez & Alessi, 2012; Chuang, 2015; Coghlan & Wylie, 2011; Cunningham & DeMarni Cromer, 2016; Farrell & Fahy, 2009; Feingold, 2005; McAdam, 2013; Meshkovska, Mickovski, Bos, & Siegel, 2016; Piper et al., 2015; Sanford et al., 2016; Segrave, 2009; Sharma, 2005; Stepnitz, 2012; Szörényi & Eate, 2014; Wijers, 2015; Wilson & O'Brien, 2016, p. 41). In fact, Kelly (2005, p. 243) estimates that only half of those who need assistance actually receive it.

The Victim Hierarchy

The problem of this stereotyping is that it creates a scale against which the affected are measured. As a result, even when recognised as victims, non- or less-ideal, but no less real ones, are either offered less support, or denied any altogether. Individuals denied victimhood include those victims trafficked by people they know, which in reality includes a sizeable proportion of total victims (Marchionni, 2012; Sharma, 2005).

One requirement is for the victim to have done nothing that can be considered as having contributed to their being trafficked. This means that if one wishes to be seen as a victim, one must deny all agency. Once a person is a designated 'victim', their agency is also not acknowledged in subsequent proceedings, as victims are presumed unable to speak for themselves (De Shalit et al., 2014; Dijk, 2013; Sobel, 2016). Even more so, the characteristic of lacking agency and having victim-status are circular; Alvarez and Alessi (2012), Chuang (2015), and Columb (2015) suggest that the victim-status itself implies a lack of agency, while the (assumed) lack of agency facilitates victim-status.

Particularly problematic is the gendered interpretation of who can and cannot consent to their movement and exploitation, which relates to the gendered assumption of who can and cannot be deemed a victim, and is not unrelated to cultural constructions of men as active and women as passive (see Marchionni, 2012; Wylie, 2016): women are constructed as victims of male sexual violence (Hua & Nigorizawa, 2010).

Criminalisation

Those who fail to qualify as victims are not just denied support and sympathy. They are often criminalised, even though Aronowitz's (2009, p. xii) exposition highlights the need to approach all trafficked/smuggled people as the victims they are. Stigmatisation and criminalisation occur both informally and formally.

Informally, socially, many less-ideal victims find themselves blamed for their own victimisation, stigmatised, and even ostracised. Such responses are relatively constant across nations. Buckley (2009) indicates that previous research on Russian responses to victims of trafficking indicates that these victims are rejected by their families and communities. Cunningham and DeMarni Cromer (2016) show that US males also tend to blame victims. In Krsmanovic's (2016, pp. 159–160) article engaging with Serbian newspaper texts about sex trafficking, photography serves to simplify the matter of trafficking and dehumanise, even blame the victim, either for her naiveté, or her willing engagement in the sex industry. Even when the victim is not explicitly blamed, Sobel (2016) suggests that by not mentioning the trafficker, victims are implicitly held responsible for their victimisation.

Formal responses often go beyond simple victim-blaming. For instance, the US Trafficking and Violence Protection Act (TVPA) distinguishes between 'good' victims (of trafficking), and 'bad' victims (of smuggling). As a result of this Act, the voluntarily smuggled worker is criminalised, whereas the supposedly involuntarily trafficked slave is considered a victim (Hua & Nigorizawa, 2010, pp. 406–407), despite the fact that many smuggled workers end up exploited upon arrival, and are often deceived or coerced into this exploitation (meaning that, legally, they become victims of trafficking). As Hua and Nigorizawa (2010, p. 407) put it:

> Trafficking cases [...] may involve many potential victims, but only those who are able to prove their authenticity by fitting into pre-existing assumptions tied to the category 'trafficked victim' are officially granted victim status. Similar to other immigration practices, the TVPA continues in a tradition where 'worthy victims' are sorted from complicit and therefore illegal immigrants.

Columb (2015) shows that organ donors who are not recognised as organ trafficking victims are criminalised by the international protocols on the organ trade. In one case, the judges acknowledged the victim's exploitation and even note 'the suspect had been trafficked', but sentenced them regardless (Anti-Slavery International, 2014, p. 30). Generally, people who have, whether voluntarily or involuntarily, been moved across borders are, if not recognised as victims of trafficking, branded illegal migrants, and as a result criminalised.

As the Anti-Slavery International (2014) report also suggests, misidentifying victims as offenders not only generates secondary victimisation and vulnerability (with victims having a criminal record and being at an increased risk of going 'missing', deportation, and re-trafficking). It also generates fear of the authorities, reducing the victim's cooperativeness and assistance with further investigations. Criminalisation often has the effect of making victims' situations more precarious by putting them at risk of arrest and prosecution, enhancing exploiters' and traffickers' hold over them (Feingold, 2005; Kelly, 2005; Sharma, 2005; Weitzer, 2007).

Secondary Victimisation

Even if the victim is successfully recognised as such, and even if practitioners are suitably trained and sufficiently supportive during their 'rescue', many legal systems entail (unintentional) secondary victimisation. For instance, police raids of sex workplaces are violent, traumatising events, harming possible survivors of sex trafficking through interrogation, detention, prosecution, and deportation (Hill, 2016, p. 46). Where sex workers are being 'rescued' by police, '[f]orce, it seems, has become protection, just as war became peace, slavery freedom and ignorance strength, in George Orwell's *1984*' (O'Connell Davidson, 2015, p. 205).

Further secondary victimisation occurs after the 'rescue', during the investigation and prosecution, by forcing witnesses and victims to re-live traumatic experiences through repeated interview/interrogation and testifying in court (Meshkovska et al., 2016; Wijers, 2015). Police and judges are often insufficiently trained to understand and respond to the primary trauma suffered by victims (Dijk, 2013; Meshkovska et al., 2016), leading to (unintentionally) harmful practices. The burden of proof is on the prosecuting party, meaning that victims' testimony is put under thorough scrutiny by the defending party (Meshkovska et al., 2016). Criminal proceedings may take years (Meshkovska et al., 2016), during which the victim lives in a state of uncertainty about their legal (immigration) status, and they do not automatically receive compensation from those successfully prosecuted as traffickers. In fact, in order to receive compensation, the victim would have to initiate civil proceedings, which entails another long and arduous legal process (Meshkovska et al., 2016).

Regardless of whether a victim is successfully recognised as a victim and is successfully used by the state in prosecuting traffickers, state responses often include repatriation (Dijk, 2013; Wijers, 2015). This often puts victims in the same situation they (were) moved from in the first place (Feingold, 2005), but with additional stigma and possible debt (Kelly, 2005), thereby increasing their vulnerability and the likelihood of their being re-trafficked.

SOCIO-POLITICAL CAUSES AND EFFECTS OF MISREPRESENTATION

The modern slavery narrative is simplistic and fairy-tale-like, a narrative of good and bad. While simplifying complex events is essential in raising the news value of a story (Galtung & Ruge, 1965; Jewkes, 2011), the harmful effects are numerous. As the earlier section shows, many truly affected persons are, as a result of the victimhood-threshold sustained by the narrative, not offered sufficient support. Wylie (2016) describes in much detail the interests of both global and local parties in adopting and perpetuating this oversimplified and misdirected narrative, which include material power, soft power, and a perpetuation of other norms such as those relating to gender/sex.

The Focus on Female Victims and Sex Trafficking

The HT narrative sustains gender inequality by perpetuating the myth that men act and women are acted upon (Sobel, 2016; Szörényi & Eate, 2014; Wylie, 2016). Women are vulnerable, naïve victims, who must be saved by heroic (male) saviours. This gender bias can be traced back to the historical 'white slavery' campaign (Farrell & Fahy, 2009; Krsmanovic, 2016; Lobasz, 2009) and to cultural attitudes toward female empowerment and sexuality (Attwood, 2016; Hall, 2015; Szörényi & Eate, 2014).

Those parts of the story that are most illustrative of these sexist attitudes focus on female victims of sexual exploitation. Not only does this focus reiterate the notion that victims are primarily female, that is, women are acted upon, but it is also indicative of a male gaze, whereby women's bodies are objectified as instruments of (male) sexual thrill, not just directly through the sexual abuse of these bodies, but also through the titillating reporting of this abuse.

Through this narrative, it is suggested that the safest place for a woman is to remain at home and to not undertake any supposed risky activities in the pursuit of a better future. This is also evident in counter-trafficking campaigns' exaggeration of the perils of migration, which indeed 'advocate the private sphere as the safest location for [particularly] women' (Andrijasevic, 2007, p. 41). These narratives are reminiscent of children's literature, where 'home' is seen as the place where we ought to stay or come back to, as opposed to adult literature which sees home as the place we must escape or grow away from (see Clausen 1982, p. 142).

Female migrants are not the only ones held back by this narrative. While female migrants are perceived as trafficked, subsequently stigmatised, and often deported after being used to prosecute their traffickers, male migrants are either perceived as traffickers, or as voluntarily smuggled, criminalised, and then similarly deported after prosecution.

The Lack of Focus on Labour Trafficking and Domestic Trafficking

The needs of victims (both of trafficking and of global inequality) are secondary to the needs of those with vested interests in maintaining a status quo (Segrave, 2009), such as the ready supply of cheap, exploitable labour. (Western) individuals and states benefit from the current narrative of HT, which glosses over the topic of labour exploitation by focusing on sex trafficking instead (Wylie, 2016). Labour trafficking enables the exploitation of the global poor, which results in lower prices (Szörényi, 2016). There is a general lack of attention to consumers demanding cheap products, thereby increasing demand for cheap labour (Kara, 2010; Mendel & Sharapov, 2016; O'Brien, 2016).

Global wealth inequality is one of the main structural causes of trafficking. Globalisation has led to global wealth and inequality having become more visible, meaning that the desire to migrate has also increased (Russell, 2014, p. 537). As migrants have relatively few options, they often have no choice but to engage in exploitative labour in order to survive (Lewis & Waite, 2015, p. 3). Indeed, many HT victims are undocumented migrants (Lobasz, 2009, p. 327). In other words, the current version of the story of human trafficking is used to justify policing the (transnational) movement of the dispossessed when politically expedient (Sharma, 2005), but simultaneously glosses over those forms of trafficking that serve Western interests (Wylie, 2016).

Addressing gender inequality is politically and ideologically difficult, as is also evidenced by broader ongoing struggles for gender equality. Similarly, relieving poverty and insecurity of those people at risk of trafficking and smuggling would result in a more empowered and less desperate workforce, which would diminish global inequality. In turn, many currently powerful parties, both as nations and as individuals, would lose their ability to exploit this workforce.

Global and Local Politics (as Cause and Effect)

In both the USA and the UK, the anti-HT discourse constructs trafficking as an imported problem and often criminalises all transnational movement except of the most 'worthy' (Sharma, 2005; Andrijasevic, 2007, p. 43; Wylie, 2016), legitimising strict border control and migration policies (Wylie, 2016). However, Kara (2010, p. 117) warns that creating tougher laws pushes trafficking and smuggling further underground, increasing victim vulnerability. At the same time, 'tough' border control and migration policies are seen as vote winning, as is also evident in the popularity of border control television programmes (Szörényi, 2016, p. 86). Wylie (2016) traces the popularity of border control to the need for national governments to signal control in a globalising and globalised world.

Furthermore, the characterisation of trafficking as a foreign and imported problem distracts from the fact that many local causes of trafficking (e.g., poverty, conflict) are the result of the foreign policies of countries such as the USA and the UK. Through foreign policies specifically aimed at 'combating' trafficking, such as the USA's TVPA, these nations are able to maintain the illusion of being 'the good guys' (Wylie, 2016). In awareness campaigns, too, developed nations are positioned as the 'powerful saviour, rather than recognising any impact that developed economies may have in causing or perpetuating systems of global inequality' (O'Brien, 2016, p. 216; see also Pajnik's 2010 media framing analysis' similar finding). As Wilson and O'Brien (2016, p. 42) put it,

> [t]hrough constructing the victims of human trafficking as entirely passive actors that lack rational agency, states can position themselves as patriarchal protectors of the weak and innocent, thereby expanding their internal and external policing powers [which] allows wealthy states to maintain the global imbalance of economic and political capital, as human migration from impoverished states to wealthy states is conflated with human trafficking via a fantastical narrative of deception and exploitation.

Rather than addressing their responsibilities in terms of re-evaluating damaging foreign policies, these nations focus on the type of symptom control that appears well-intentioned. Ultimately, this focus results in the re-victimisation of affected people, while this re-victimisation results in perpetuating the inequalities from which these nations benefit. In other words, other versions of the story of human trafficking, that would perhaps focus more on labour trafficking, might result in the examination of the global socio-economic and political inequalities and the supply of cheap(er) labour that benefits these countries, which would be contrary to their interests. It is, indeed, also these states that most intensely reproduce and police the currently dominant version of the story of human trafficking.

Perhaps the most powerful tool in actually maintaining this story, and thereby economic and gender inequalities, is the USA's Trafficking Victims Protection Act (see Wylie, 2016). The TVPA is used to award, and penalise, nations and NGOs who either support and follow, or fail to follow, the USA's conception of what trafficking entails, and which measures are supposed to be taken to fight it (Cojocaru, 2016; Dijk, 2013; Hua & Nigorizawa, 2010; Small, 2012; Snajdr, 2013; Weitzer, 2007; Wilson & O'Brien, 2016). A number of analysts (Cojocaru, 2016; Farrell & Fahy, 2009; Hall, 2015; Lobasz, 2009; Marchionni, 2012; O'Brien, 2016; Small, 2012; Weitzer, 2007) state that the TVPA in turn is influenced by what they argue is the alliance between certain right-wing Christian groups and conservative-abolitionist feminist groups, and that this alliance is based on a consideration that all sex work is inherently problematic. Wylie (2016) indeed traces the current version of the story of HT, which focuses on sex trafficking of women and children, to the activism of this unlikely alliance united in the pursuit of the abolition of prostitution. The USA use their economic power to impose, narrowly, their narrative of HT, and broadly, a gender-related ideology, upon other actors (Wylie, 2016). A vivid example is Howard's (2012) ethnographic case study of trafficking in Benin. Though acknowledging that global economic inequality is an important trafficking structural factor in trafficking, addressing it would mean that local NGOs would lose their US (-backed) funding, and Benin would suffer politically (Howard, 2012).

In short, the story of HT has political use. The 'heroism' of 'saviours' identifies certain states, such as the USA, as the 'good guys', legitimated by their pursuit of alleviating the 'plight' of certain 'victims', conveniently glossing over the structural and global factors that put certain populations at a higher risk of exploitation than others (Alvarez & Alessi, 2012; Johnston et al., 2015; Szörényi & Eate, 2014; Weitzer, 2007; Wylie, 2016) and maintaining the economic benefits of having an exploitable, dispossessed workforce that can be policed when it is politically expedient to do so.

Secondary Exploitation

(Western) nations, consumers and employers are not the only ones benefiting from perpetuating the factors that put people at risk of trafficking. Wylie (2016, pp. 7–9) describes the vast range of institutions that have been tasked, or have tasked themselves, with responding to human trafficking. These exist on levels varying from the local to the supra-national, and include bureaucratic, non-profit, and academic institutions (ibid.). They benefit both monetarily and socially. They are, for instance, rewarded for their adoption of the 'saviour' role (Cojocaru, 2016; Hoefinger, 2016; Steele, 2015). This role allows them to advance their careers and social status, and, in the case of NGOs, continue to receive funding from, among others, the US government (Cojocaru, 2016). One particularly overt form of this 'secondary exploitation' (Cojocaru, 2016) is described by Bernstein and Shih (2014) in their ethnographical account of a *for-profit* 'reality tour' organised by two anti-trafficking organisations to enable (Western) tourists to visit and explore (and be seen to condemn) the Thai sex industry.

CONCLUSION

As this introduction has shown, only those who fulfil a very strict set of requirements are successfully identified as victims in contemporary anti-trafficking discourse. They must be female, young, preferably exploited in the sex trade, and moved without consent. This (very high) threshold means that many real victims are unrecognised, and as a result do not receive the appropriate support. In fact, they are often criminalised.

The main problem with this story is that it distracts from the structural factors that put people at risk of being trafficked, such as poverty and the global demand for cheap labour. As a result, the global West maintains its economically and ideologically dominant position and maintains existing gender norms (and thereby gender inequalities). These inequalities are, in a circular fashion, also at the root of trafficking. In short, the representation of trafficking does not aim to eradicate trafficking—it is a key factor in its perpetuation.

In this Collection

Given the contemporaneous nature of this project, the studies that follow all utilised material produced after 2000, and material consistent with the HT definition previously outlined.

Gregoriou and Ras's chapter (Chap. 2) draws on corpus linguistic analysis of a 61.5-million-word corpus of UK news texts published during 2000–2016, and on qualitative critical discourse analysis of a 67-article sub-corpus thereof. Both approaches analyse naming strategies, metaphors, grammar, and participants' speech, though the sub-corpus analysis also engages with the accompanying images multimodally. Our findings show an over-reporting of sexual exploitation, and an insistence on victims being young, female, and vulnerable. As a result, non-stereotypical victims of crimes like forced begging and domestic servitude are not readily recognised as victims and are deprived of opportunities for assistance.

Muždeka's chapter (Chap. 3) compares the representation of transnational HT in news media texts in English and Serbian by adopting contemporary narrative, cultural, and media theory. The second chapter's UK sample corpus is here compared with a similarly compiled corpus of Serbian human trafficking news texts. It is worth comparing these two differing countries' outputs; unlike the UK, which serves as a HT destination country, Serbia serves as a country of origin, a destination country, and a key transit country in the Balkans, and lies on the route of refugees from the Middle East. Differences and similarities in representations between these two countries can highlight the roles of national politics, economics, and the realities of HT in shaping the narrative. This chapter's analysis identifies the narrative strategies (pertaining to the text, story, fabula, authorship, voice, and ideological positioning) that not only shape the news media texts but also function as a semiotic code through which reality is itself constructed. The chapter explores the construction of meaning as a socially and culturally conditioned process due to which particular aspects of transnational HT are prioritised (i.e., use of official sources), while other are neglected and/or completely excluded (i.e., victims' future), thus influencing the public perception and responses.

Beyer (Chap. 4) uses British and Scandinavian crime fiction to investigate the social implications of illegal movements of people, including Transnational Human Trafficking (THT), into Western Europe, specifically focusing on transnational child trafficking (TCT) and its representation. The inclusion of Scandinavian crime fiction in this analysis is crucial to its findings. Post-2000 Danish crime fiction has been actively at the forefront of treating social realist themes such as human trafficking and modern slavery (Brunsdale, 2016), and these trends extend to Swedish and British crime fiction. British and Scandinavian crime novels are employed in Beyer's analysis to demonstrate how countries, which are differently positioned geographically, are affected by HT from the Global South and in the aftermath of the fall of the Eastern Bloc, and specifically how their national crime literatures absorb and represent the theme of HT. The chapter argues that crime fiction can be seen to engage explicitly in public and private debates around HT, and effect change, and that this didactic dimension demonstrates the power of genre fiction not merely to entertain, but also importantly to heighten awareness and open up new debates.

Dearey (Chap. 5) analyses and interrogates the identities of 'traffickers' as represented within a series of television documentaries on modern slavery. The subject of analysis is specifically to depart from the UK/'Western' view or gaze and to consider the perspective from the global East/South. That this series is presented by Al Jazeera English and by a former BBC presenter who is of Muslim origin adds further dimensionality to this text. Furthermore, the types of human trafficking featured, as well as traffickers and victims, span the globe. Analysis of trafficker identities within the different typologies represented in the documentary series are shown— bridal, charcoal, prison, sex, food, child, bonded slavery/trafficking. These are represented within a complex geo-cultural televisual gaze (Al Jazeera English) upon the global north/west as ultimately the source of the slavery problem.

REFERENCES

Alvarez, M. B., & Alessi, E. J. (2012). Human trafficking is more than sex trafficking and prostitution: Implications for social work. *Affilia, 27*(2), 142–152.
Andrijasevic, R. (2007). Beautiful dead bodies: Gender, migration and representation in anti-trafficking campaigns. *Feminist Review, 86,* 24–44.
Andrijasevic, R., & Mai, N. (2016). Editorial: Trafficking (in) representations: Understanding the recurring appeal of victimhood and slavery in neoliberal times. *Anti-Trafficking Review, 7,* 1–10.
Anti-Slavery International. (2014). *Trafficking for forced criminal activities and begging in Europe.* [Online]. Retrieved November 2016, from http://freedomfund.org/wp-content/uploads/race_report_english.pdf

Aronowitz, A. (2009). *Human trafficking, human misery: The global trade in human beings.* London: Greenwood Publishing Group.

Attwood, R. (2016). Looking beyond 'white slavery': Trafficking, the Jewish Association, and the dangerous politics of migration control in England, 1890–1910. *Anti-Trafficking Review, 7,* 115–138.

Avendaño, A., & Fanning, C. (2013). Immigration policy reform in the United States: Reframing the enforcement discourse to fight human trafficking and promote shared prosperity. *Anti-Trafficking Review, 2,* 97–118.

Bernstein, E., & Shih, E. (2014). The erotics of authenticity: Sex trafficking and 'reality tourism' in Thailand. *Social Politics: International Studies in Gender, State and Society, 21*(3), 430–460.

Brunsdale, M. M. (2016). *Encyclopedia of Nordic crime fiction: Works and authors of Denmark, Finland, Norway and Sweden since 1967.* Jefferson: McFarland.

Buckley, M. (2009). Public opinion in Russia on the politics of human trafficking. *Europe-Asia Studies, 61*(2), 213–248.

Christie, N. (1986). The ideal victim. In E. A. Fattah (ed.), *From crime policy to victim policy.* London: Palgrave Macmillan.

Chuang, J. (2015). The challenges and perils of reframing trafficking as 'modern-day slavery'. *Anti-Trafficking Review, 5,* 146–149.

Clausen, C. (1982). Home and away in children's fiction. *Children's Literature, 10,* 141–152.

Coghlan, D., & Wylie, G. (2011). Defining trafficking/denying justice? Forced labour in Ireland and the consequences of trafficking discourse. *Journal of Ethnic and Migration Studies, 37*(9), 1513–1526.

Cojocaru, C. (2016). My experience is mine to tell: Challenging the abolitionist victimhood framework. *Anti-Trafficking Review, 7,* 12–38.

Columb, S. (2015). Beneath the organ trade: A critical analysis of the organ trafficking discourse. *Crime, Law and Social Change, 63*(1), 21–47.

Cunningham, K., & DeMarni Cromer, L. (2016). Attitudes about human trafficking: Individual differences related to belief and victim blame. *Journal of Interpersonal Violence, 31*(2), 228–244.

Dando, C. J., Walsh, D., & Brierley, R. (2016). Perceptions of psychological coercion and human trafficking in the West Midlands of England: Beginning to know the unknown. *PLoS ONE, 11*(5), 1–13.

De Shalit, A., Heynen, R., & Van der Meulen, E. (2014). Human trafficking and media myths: Federal funding, communication strategies, and Canadian anti-trafficking programs. *Canadian Journal of Communication, 39*(3), 385–412.

De Villiers, N. (2016). Rebooting trafficking. *Anti-Trafficking Review,* (7), 161–181.

Denton, E. (2010). International news coverage of human trafficking arrests and prosecutions: A content analysis. *Women & Criminal Justice, 20*(1–2), 10–26.

Dijk, A. M. (2013). Combating human trafficking in Poland: When victims are lost in translation. *Washington University Global Studies Law Review, 12*(4), 783–806.

Duong, K. A. (2014). Human trafficking in a globalized world: Gender aspects of the issue and anti-trafficking politics. *Journal of Research in Gender Studies,* 4(1), 788–805.

European Commission. (2017). *European civil protection and humanitarian aid operations: Serbia, facts figures.* [Online]. European Commission. Retrieved February, 11, 2017, from http://ec.europa.eu/echo/files/aid/countries/factsheets/serbia_en.pdf

Farrell, A., & Fahy, S. (2009). The problem of human trafficking in the U.S: Public frames and policy responses. *Journal of Criminal Justice, 37*(6), 617–626.

Feingold, D. A. (2005). Human trafficking. *Foreign Policy, 150,* 26–32.

Finnemore, M., & Sikkink, K. (1998). International norm dynamics and political change. *International Organization, 52*(4), 887–917.

Galtung, J., & Ruge, M. (1965). Structuring and selecting news. In S. Cohen & J. Young (eds.), *The manufacture of news: Social problems, deviance and the mass media* (Revised ed., pp. 52–63). London: Constable.

Gould, C. (2010). Moral panic, human trafficking and the 2010 Soccer World Cup. *Agenda, 24*(85), 31–44.

Hall, S. L. (2015). The uncanny sacrifice: Sex trafficking in Chris Abani's *Becoming Abigail. Critique—Bolingbroke Society, 56*(1), 42–60.

Haynes, D. F. (2014). The celebritization of human trafficking. *The Annals of the American Academy of Social and Political Science, 653*(1), 25–45.

Hill, A. (2016). How to stage a raid: Police, media and the master narrative of trafficking. *Anti-Trafficking Review, 7,* 39–55.

Hoefinger, H. (2016). Neoliberal sexual humanitarianism and story-telling: The case of Somaly Mam. *Anti-Trafficking Review, 7,* 56–78.

Howard, N. (2012). Accountable to whom? Accountable for what? Understanding anti-child trafficking discourse and policy in Southern Benin. *Anti-Trafficking Review, 1,* 43–59.

Hua, J., & Nigorizawa, H. (2010). US sex trafficking, women's human rights and the politics of representation. *International Feminist Journal of Politics, 12*(3–4), 401–423.

Jewkes, Y. (2011). *Media and crime* (2nd ed.). London: Sage.

Johnston, A., Friedman, B., & Sobel, M. (2015). Framing an emerging issue: How U.S. print and broadcast news media covered sex trafficking, 2008–2012. *Journal of Human Trafficking, 1*(3), 235–254.

Kara, S. (2010). *Sex trafficking: Inside the business of modern slavery.* New York: Columbia University Press.

Kelly, L. (2005). 'You can find anything you want': A critical reflection on research on trafficking in persons within and into Europe. *International Migration, 43*(1–2), 235–265.

Kinney, E. (2015). Victims, villains, and valiant rescuers: Unpacking sociolegal constructions of human trafficking and crimmigration in popular culture. In

M. J. Guia (ed.), *The illegal business of human trafficking* (pp. 87–108). Cham: Springer.

Krsmanovic, E. (2016). Captured 'Realities' of human trafficking: Analysis of photographs illustrating stories on trafficking into the sex industry in Serbian media. *Anti-Trafficking Review, 7*, 139–160.

Lewis, H., & Waite, L. (2015). Asylum, immigration restrictions and exploitation: Hyper-precarity as a lens for understanding and tackling forced labour. *Anti-Trafficking Review, 5*, 50–68.

Limoncelli, S. A. (2009). The trouble with trafficking: Conceptualising women's sexual labor and economic human rights. *Women's Studies International Forum, 32*, 261–269.

Lobasz, J. K. (2009). Beyond border security: Feminist approaches to human trafficking. *Security Studies, 18*(2), 319–144.

Marchionni, D. M. (2012). International human trafficking: An agenda-building analysis of the US and British Press. *International Communication Gazette, 74*(2), 145–158.

McAdam, M. (2013). Who's who at the border? A rights-based approach to identifying human trafficking at international borders. *Anti-Trafficking Review, 2*, 33–49.

Mendel, J., & Sharapov, K. (2016). Human trafficking and online networks: Policy, analysis, and ignorance. *Antipode: A Radical Journal of Geography, 48*(3), 665–684.

Meshkovska, B., Mickovski, N., Bos, A. E. R., & Siegel, M. (2016). Trafficking of women for sexual exploitation in Europe: Prosecution, trials and their impact. *Anti-Trafficking Review, 6*, 71–90.

Moore, A. S., & Goldberg, E. S. (2015). Victims, perpetrators, and the limits of human rights discourse in post-Palermo fiction about sex trafficking. *The International Journal of Human Rights, 19*(1), 16–31.

Musto, J. L. (2009). What's in a name? Conflations and contradictions in contemporary U.S. discourses of human trafficking. *Women's Studies International Forum, 32*(4), 281–287.

O'Brien, E. (2016). Human trafficking heroes and villains: Representing the problem in anti-trafficking awareness campaigns. *Social & Legal Studies, 25*(2), 205–224.

O'Connell Davidson, J. (2010). New slavery, old binaries: Human trafficking and the borders of 'freedom'. *Global Networks, 10*(2), 244–261.

O'Connell Davidson, J. (2015). *Modern slavery: The margins of freedom.* Basingstoke: Palgrave Macmillan.

Pajnik, M. (2010). Media framing of trafficking. *International Feminist Journal of Politics, 12*(1), 45–64.

Papadouka, M. E., Evangelopoulos, N., & Ignatow, G. (2016). Agenda setting and active audiences in online coverage of human trafficking. *Information, Communication & Society, 19*(5), 655–672.

Piper, N., Segrave, M., & Napier-Moore, R. (2015). Editorial: What's in a name? Distinguishing forced labour, trafficking and slavery. *Anti-Trafficking Review, 5,* 1–9.

Plambech, S. (2016). The art of the possible: Making films on sex work migration and human trafficking. *Anti-Trafficking Review, 7,* 182–199.

Russell, A. M. (2014). Victims of trafficking: The feminisation of poverty and migration in the gendered narratives of human trafficking. *Societies, 4*(4), 532–548.

Sanchez, G. (2016). 'It's All in Their Brain': Constructing the figure of the trafficking victim on the US-Mexico border. *Anti-Trafficking Review, 7,* 97–114.

Sanford, R., Martínez, D. E., & Weitzer, R. (2016). Framing human trafficking: A content analysis of recent U.S. newspaper articles. *Journal of Human Trafficking, 2*(2), 139–155.

Segrave, M. (2009). Order at the border: The repatriation of victims of trafficking. *Women's Studies International Forum, 32,* 251–260.

Sharma, N. (2005). Anti-trafficking rhetoric and the making of a global apartheid. *NWSA Journal, 17,* 88–111.

Small, J. L. (2012). Trafficking in truth: Media, sexuality, and human rights evidence. *Feminist Studies, 38*(2), 415–443.

Snajdr, E. (2013). Beneath the master narrative: Human trafficking, myths of sexual slavery and ethnographic realities. *Dialectical Anthropology, 37*(2), 229–256.

Sobel, M. R. (2014). Chronicling a crisis: Media framing of human trafficking in India, Thailand, and the USA. *Asian Journal of Communication, 24*(4), 315–332.

Sobel, M. R. (2016). Confronting sex trafficking: Gender depictions in newspaper coverage from the former Soviet republics and the Baltic states. *European Journal of Communication, 31*(2), 152–168.

Steele, S. L. (2015). Real and unreal masculinities: The celebrity image in anti-trafficking campaigns. *Journal of Gender Studies, 24*(4), 419–435.

Stepnitz, A. (2012). A lie more disastrous than the truth: Asylum and the identification of trafficked women in the UK. *Anti-Trafficking Review, 1,* 104–121.

Szörényi, A. (2016). Expelling slavery from the nation: Representations of labour exploitation in Australia's supply chain. *Anti-Trafficking Review, 7,* 79–96.

Szörényi, A., & Eate, P. (2014). Saving virgins, saving the USA: Heteronormative masculinities and the securitisation of trafficking discourse in mainstream narrative film. *Social Semiotics, 24*(5), 608–622.

Van der Pijl, Y., Oude Breuil, B. C., & Siegel, D. (2011). Is there such thing as 'global sex trafficking'? A patchwork tale on useful (mis)understandings. *Crime, Law and Social Change, 56*(5), 567–582.

Weitzer, R. (2007). The social construction of sex trafficking: Ideology and institutionalisation of a moral crusade. *Politics and Society, 35,* 447–475.

Wijers, M. (2015). Purity, victimhood and agency: Fifteen years of the UN trafficking protocol. *Anti-Trafficking Review, 4,* 56–79.

Wilson, M., & O'Brien, E. (2016). Constructing the ideal victim in the United States of America's annual trafficking in persons reports. *Crime, Law and Social Change, 65*(1), 29–45.

Winterdyk, J., Reichel, P., & Perrin, B. (eds.). (2012). *Human trafficking: Exploring the international nature, concerns, and complexities.* Boca Raton: CRC Press.

Wylie, G. (2016). *The international politics of human trafficking.* London: Palgrave.

Yick, A. G. (2010). Social construction of human trafficking on YouTube: An exploratory study. *Journal of Immigrant & Refugee Studies, 8*(1), 11–16.

CHAPTER 2

'Call for Purge on the People Traffickers': An Investigation into British Newspapers' Representation of Transnational Human Trafficking, 2000–2016

Christiana Gregoriou and Ilse A. Ras

Abstract Gregoriou and Ras draw on corpus linguistics and critical discourse analysis to examine a 61.5 million-word corpus of articles published by UK newspapers between 2000 and 2016, and on qualitative critical discourse analysis of a sixty-seven-article sample corpus in depth. Both approaches analyse the naming and describing of victims and traffickers, metaphors, transitivity, and speech and writing presentation, while the in-depth qualitative approach furthermore analyses the text (images) (multi)modally. Their findings conclude that trafficking for sexual exploitation is over-reported compared to other forms of trafficking, and that victims are generally presented as young, female, and vulnerable. As a result, non-stereotypical victims, of crimes like forced begging and domestic servitude, are not readily recognised as victims, and thereby are deprived of opportunities for assistance.

C. Gregoriou (✉) • I. A. Ras
School of English, University of Leeds, Leeds, UK
e-mail: c.gregoriou@leeds.ac.uk; i.a.ras@leeds.ac.uk

© The Author(s) 2018
C. Gregoriou (ed.), *Representations of Transnational Human Trafficking*, https://doi.org/10.1007/978-3-319-78214-0_2

Keywords Critical discourse analysis • Corpus linguistics • Human trafficking • Newspapers • Transnational organised crime

INTRODUCTION

To analyse UK media representations of human trafficking (henceforth HT), certain research questions must be answered. How are trafficking, traffickers, and HT victims represented, and to what extent are victims criminalised and victimised,[1] sex trafficking overrepresented, and smuggling and trafficking conflated by the UK press? Such overarching research questions are designed to shed light on underlying ideologies relating to agency, responsibility, and vulnerability, and will respectively guide the critical discourse analysis of the whole corpus[2] (quantitatively) and the spike sample corpus (qualitatively).

DATA COLLECTION

Given the 'present day' focus of this project, the time frame was restricted to 2000–2016; we focus on UK articles published after 2000 as this was the year of the ratification of the Palermo Protocol.[3] This 16-year period also covers the years running up to the UK Parliament passing the Modern Slavery Act 2015, which defines HT, slavery, and exploitation as applicable to the English and Welsh criminal justice system. The dataset was limited to UK national daily and Sunday newspapers alone.

To address corpus compilation considerations with regard to the relevance of the included texts and the exhaustiveness of the corpus, we drew on Gabrielatos' (2007) data collection method, which he developed as

[1] We distinguish primary victimisation (which directly affects the victim) from secondary victimisation (such as in the form of victim blaming), re-victimisation (such as falling victim to re-trafficking), indirect victimisation (such as with reference to detrimental effects on one's family) and secondary exploitation (in the form of anyone benefitting from the problem's existence).
[2] 'A corpus is a collection of pieces of language text in electronic form, selected according to external criteria to represent, as far as possible, a language or language variety as a source of data for linguistic research' (Sinclair, 2005).
[3] United Nation's *Protocol to Prevent, Suppress and Punish Trafficking in Persons Especially Women and Children, supplementing the United Nations Convention against Transnational Organized Crime* (UNODC, 2016).

part of a research project examining UK media representations of refugees, asylum seekers, and (im)migrants. Our resultant search terms were: *bonded labour, child labour, debt bondage, domestic servitude, exploitation, exploitative labour, forced criminality, forced labour, forced prostitution, human trafficker, human trafficking, labour trafficking, organ harvesting, raid-and-rescue, sex slave, sex slaves, sex trafficking, sexual exploitation, sexual servitude, slave, slave trade, slaves, trafficked, trafficked victims, traffickers, trafficking (in/of) persons, trafficking (in/of) human being/s,* and *woman trafficking.*[4]

The Corpus

Our method generated a resulting corpus of 80,608 articles. It contains 61,571,641 tokens (as in 'words') and 388,834 types (of words). As Table 2.1 shows, relatively large numbers of articles were published in *The Guardian, The Times* and *The Independent,* which suggests that results are skewed toward the representation of HT by British broadsheets. As such, the corpus is not representative of what the British public *reads* about HT, but of what the British press *writes* about HT.

---

[4] Gabrielatos' (2007) method works by first selecting a limited set of search terms that are then used to generate several sample corpora. Our initial search terms were *human trafficking, human trafficker, trafficking* (in/of) *human being/s, slavery, sexual exploitation, sex trafficking, sexual trafficking, sex slave,* and *forced labour.* We first collected sample corpora (i.e., a selection of the intended final, full corpus) from Lexis Nexis for the periods 1/1/2000–30/9/2000, 1/1/2008–30/9/2008, and 1/1/2016–30/9/2016, to ensure that our results would not be unduly skewed toward either end, or indeed the middle, of the overall time frame. Each initial sample corpus was then uploaded to Wmatrix (Rayson, 2009) and compared to a reference corpus (a corpus that serves as the benchmark against which the primary corpus is, or our sample corpora were, compared), which in our case was the BNC Written Sampler (a corpus intended to be representative of written British English), to generate three keyword (words used significantly less or more often in the primary corpus than in the reference corpus) lists, one for each sample corpus, which were then combined. The potential usefulness of each keyword was evaluated by calculating RQTR scores (a mathematical measure indicating the potential relevance of a keyword as a search term) following Gabrielatos (2007). Further potential search terms were selected introspectively by members of the project team, based on their reading of the relevant literature. These potential search terms were also evaluated using Gabrielatos' (2007) RQTR score. It was the resultant list of search terms that was used to collect articles from Lexis Nexis over the full time frame 1/1/2000–30/9/2016.

Table 2.1   Number of human trafficking-related articles published by UK newspapers between 01/2000 and 09/2016

Newspaper	Articles
Business	62
Daily Edition	180
Daily Mail	4,695
Daily Star	3,892
Daily Star Sunday	311
Daily Telegraph	6,151
Express	2,739
Guardian	17,127
Independent	8,187
Independent on Sunday	1,493
Mail on Sunday	1,025
Mirror	5,330
New Review	139
Observer	3,757
People	623
Saturday Magazine	19
Sun	5,879
Sunday Business	92
Sunday Express	1,050
Sunday Mirror	677
Sunday Telegraph	1,906
Sunday Times	4,806
Times	10,468
Total	80,608

Diachronic Change and Spike Sample Corpus Construction

Figure 2.1 shows that the number of articles over time has steadily climbed, which is in line with Winterdyk, Reichel, and Perrin's (2012, p. 9) notion of an 'explosion of media coverage' of HT during this time.[5]

Further to indicating that more texts were published in later years compared to the earlier ones, Fig. 2.1 also shows sizeable fluctuations in the number of articles published on HT. Even though dips in the graph are also worth examining, we here keep our focus on the graph's particularly

---

[5] The figure's vertical, y-axis, shows the number of texts generated during the period, while the horizontal, x-axis, indicates the months of each of these 16 years, from January 2000 at the far left to September 2016 at the far right. All relevant data points are accounted for in the graph, though space constraints dictate that not all month-labels are visible on the x-axis.

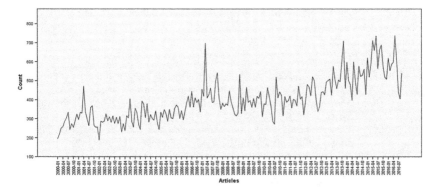

Fig. 2.1 Number of human trafficking-related articles published by UK newspapers between 01/2000 and 09/2016

large 'spikes' or increases in HT reporting, which occur in the months of April 2001, March 2007, November 2013, the summer of 2015, and May 2016. Table 2.2 shows which concurrent events are potentially associated with these spikes. Such concurrent events include the migrant crisis, certain countries joining the EU, the UK referendum and campaigns on UK membership of the EU, and (the anniversary of) events relating to HT-related legislation.

Quantitative methods of analysis are used to examine the full corpus, but qualitative methods, which are required to triangulate and complement the quantitative methods, cannot practically be used to examine a multi-million-word corpus. As such, we created another sample corpus, of prototypical[6] texts from each of these five spikes. The total number of articles in this spike sample corpus is sixty-seven.

For each spike, Table 2.3 indicates the total number of articles, the number and percentage of articles sampled, the numbers of tokens per spike, and the number and percentage of the number of words in the sample generated. As the table shows, even with our focus on spikes, and hence periods in which media reported on HT the most, our qualitative analysis was limited to 18,000 words in total, out of the 61.6 m words available. For the multimodal part of the analysis, which explores the images

---

[6] ProtAnt (Anthony, 2015) was first used to generate a list of the most prototypical articles in each spike, after which random articles were selected using Excel, to reduce each list to 1%. This percentage generated a set of sixty-seven articles, and hence a sample corpus manageable for manual analysis. For a final check, these articles were manually evaluated to ensure relevance.

Table 2.2   Events concurrent with 'spikes' in the number of human trafficking-related articles published by UK newspapers

Period	Events
April 2001	*Potentially linked to the passing of the Palermo Protocol at the end of 2000* *March*: Bomb explosion at BBC Television Centre by the new IRA *April*: Yugoslavian ex-President Milošević surrenders to be tried for war crimes
March 2007	*200 years anniversary of the abolition of the slave trade in the British Empire.* *January*: Romania and Bulgaria join the European Union *February*: ICJ finds Serbia guilty of failing to prevent Srebrenica genocide
November 2013	*150 years anniversary of the Emancipation Proclamation in the US* *April*: Boston Marathon bombing *May*: The Conservative Party publishes a draft European Union Referendum Bill *June*: Snowden leaks news of US mass surveillance operations, Murder of Lee Rigby *July*: Croatia joins the EU, President Morsi is deposed in Egypt *October*: Modern Slavery Act introduced in draft to the House of Commons *November*: President Yanukovych of Ukraine rejects closer ties to the EU Start of the Lee Rigby murder trial
Summer 2015	*European refugee crisis and Eurotunnel migrant crisis* *Daesh/ISIS continues to commit bombings and is under attack from the American, Canadian, Russian, Turkish, and Egyptian airforces.* *February*: Ceasefire is reached in Ukraine, then broken *March*: UK Modern Slavery Act becomes law *May*: UK general elections *July*: Greece misses payments to IMF, Tenth anniversary of the 7/7 attacks *September*: PM Cameron refuses to make reparations for Britain's role in the transatlantic slave trade
May 2016	*February*: PM Cameron announces that a referendum on EU membership will be held in May, Several Rotherham offenders are sentenced *March*: Brussels bombings *April*: Egypt Aircrash over the Mediterranean, Brexit campaigns start *June*: Britain votes to leave the EU

accompanying the spike sample corpus, we obtained facsimiles and online newspaper website article versions of 53,[7] (i.e., 80%), of these 67 articles.

---

[7] Facsimiles were required to facilitate a multimodal analysis of the sample corpus texts' accompanying images. Most articles were available from the British Library Newsroom in digital form, on microfilm, or in the original newspaper, although about half a dozen were

Table 2.3 Breakdown of the composition of the 'spike' sample corpora

Spike	Total articles	Articles sampled	Articles sampled (%)	Total tokens	Sample token count	Sample token percentage
April 2001	471	5	1.06	347,078	1,337	0.39
March 2007	696	7	1.01	454,288	2,465	0.54
November 2013	709	7	0.99	462,281	1,427	0.31
Summer 2015	4,060	41	1.01	3,162,473	11,277	0.36
May 2016	737	7	0.95	616,217	2,177	0.35
Corpus Total	*80,608*	*67*	*0.08*	*61,571,641*	*18,683*	*0.03*

CORPUS-ASSISTED CRITICAL DISCOURSE ANALYSIS[8]

This study examines the linguistic characteristics of UK newspaper reporting on HT that are normally also examined by critical discourse analysts/ stylisticians in relation to media texts (Fairclough, 1992; Gregoriou & Paterson, 2017; Jeffries, 2010; Mayr & Machin, 2012). Given our research questions, we prioritise the investigation of metaphors, the naming and describing of HT, its victims, traffickers, and other HT perpetrators, but also examine transitivity,[9] modality,[10] and the reporting of speech and writing. We adopted a 'mixed methods' approach by manually analysing our spike sample corpus of sixty-seven articles, supported by a corpus linguistic approach to the whole 80,608 text corpus. The qualitative analysis was conducted independently of the quantitative analysis to pre-empt the criticism of 'cherry-picking' (see Poole, 2010; Widdowson, 1995, p. 169, 1998, pp. 143–146, 2004, pp. 103–110, 157) that critical discourse analysts often face.

In metaphor, one cognitive domain is mapped against another (see Lakoff & Johnson, 1980). We adopt the traditional linguistic means of referring to metaphors using small capitals. We first focused on the spike

---

only available as online articles from the newspaper websites. A further fifteen, including nine from *The Mirror*, were simply unavailable for reasons including the fact that only one edition of a newspaper, of multiple, is actually stored and digitised by the British Library.

[8] See Baker et al. (2008, p. 295).

[9] Answering the question of who is doing what to whom/what, how and with what? (Mayr & Machin, 2012, p. 52; Richardson, 2007, p. 54).

[10] An examination of words and phrases relating to the author's notion of what is true, what is possible, and what is desirable.

sample corpus to find sustained, or mega, metaphors, and explored these further across the whole of our data set via corpus analysis, using a method similar to the one advocated by Koller, Hardie, Rayson, and Semino (2008).[11]

The corpus linguistic methods that were used to examine which topics were most important in the corpus and how various participants and concepts were (metaphorically, at times) described included the generation of a key word list.[12] These key words were subsequently categorised with the help of concordances. Categories include 'Participants', 'Acts of Abuse and Exploitation', and 'Movement'.

Various methods were used to examine the modification of the target nouns/lemmas included in this key word list. Concordance displays, c-collocate[13] lists (derived using the method set out by Gabrielatos & Baker, 2008[14]), and 2-gram lists (an *n*-gram is a word group of *n* size, and in this case we refer to word pairs) were particularly useful.

---

[11] Koller et al. (2008) take (unexpected) semantic categories, that is, groupings of broadly related words, a list of which is generated through Wmatrix, as indicative of source domains. They advocate that when source domains of interest are established prior to the examination of the corpus through Wmatrix, its 'domain push' function is used to 'push' to the foreground secondary semantic domain tags.

[12] To generate a key word list of the human trafficking news corpus, the British National Corpus Written Sampler that forms part of Wmatrix was used as a reference corpus. Two cut-off points were selected to shrink the list to a manageable length. Gabrielatos and Baker (2008) set their log-likelihood (LL; a statistical measure often used to indicate keyness) cut-off at $p < 0.000000000000001$, which they indicate as an 'extremely low' value, or an extremely high threshold. The threshold for the current key word list was set at LL > 15.13, $p < 0.001$. A further threshold of relative frequency was set, to ensure that all interpreted key words are used relatively often. Given the fact that the BNC was, at the time of the present study, 20 years old, and includes texts that are older, it is possible that certain words that are used by current-day newspapers simply did not appear in the time that many BNC texts were written.

[13] A concordance displays a word of interest in its co-text, usually 50 characters to the left and the right, for every instance of this word of interest in the corpus. A collocate is a word that occurs within a certain number of words to the left or right (usually 4 or 5) of the word of interest. Collocates of interest are those that occur at a certain (relative) frequency. A c-collocate, short for 'constant collocate', re-occurs above a certain threshold over a predefined number of years.

[14] The main issue in defining a c-collocate list is defining 'consistency'. Gabrielatos and Baker (2008) indicate that a collocate is consistent when it occurs in 7 years, at a minimum frequency of 5. As their corpus spans a decade, whereas ours spans 17 years, the minimum number of years was raised to 75%. As this, however, would mean that a collocate has to occur at least 65 times (compared to Gabrielatos and Baker's (2008) minimum overall fre-

As Jeffries (2010, p. 47) points out, through transitivity choices, the reader is presented with 'clear notions of who is in control, who is a victim and so on'. Most researchers only examine transitivity in small corpora, semi-manually.[15] As the key word analysis already distinguished between pertinent processes (e.g., acts of abuse and exploitation) and participants (e.g., survivors/victims and traffickers/offenders), this transitivity analysis focuses on a limited set of words. We took key words referring to acts of trafficking and exploitation and noted whether they are in nominalised form ('trafficking'), are past participles ('trafficked'), or have another form. We work with a more traditional understanding of transitivity (see Jeffries, 2010, p. 38), rather than Halliday's (1994) transitivity model. Our approach is, in some ways, a throwback to critical linguistics, as proposed by Fowler, Hodge, Kress, and Trew (1979), and driven primarily by the limitations of SketchEngine as experienced by us. We used SketchEngine's word sketch functionality, which shows how often a target lemma is used as a subject, as an object, and is preceded by the prepositions 'by' (for an approximation of how often lemmas were used as agents in agentive passives). For each target lemma, these frequencies were simply recorded in an Excel file. Unfortunately, word sketches cannot show how often the target lemma is used as the subject of a passive sentence. We used CQL to examine how often a target lemma was the subject of a passive sentence. In CQL, the search for a standard passive construction, [noun] [auxiliary verb (phrase)] [past participle verb], is as follows:

[lemma = "..."] [tag = "V.*"]{0,1} [tag = "VB.*"] [word = ".*d" & tag = "V.*"][16]

The query produced above was run a second time for each lemma, with the following sequence attached, to examine how often these passives included an agent[17]:

quency of 35), the minimum frequency was dropped to 3 (resulting in a minimum overall frequency of 39). Like Gabrielatos and Baker, collocates were collected from the span 5L-5R, with the target word at position 0.

[15] For instance, Rodrigues Jr. (2005), de Lima-Lopes (2014), Tabbert (2015), Bartley and Hidalgo-Tenorio (2015), and Lee (2016) manually annotate concordance lines.

[16] We acknowledge that this query only produces results for regular past participles and passive constructions created with a version of 'to be'. The best approximation of the number of agentless passives was reached by calculating the number of passive constructions that include an agent.

[17] It adds the sequence ['by' as preposition] to the original query.

[] {0,4} [word = "by" & tag = "IN"][18]

Frequencies were recorded on a year-by-year basis to facilitate future diachronic analyses, complementary to the current synchronic analysis.

As indicated, we also examine modality, the linguistic area of analysis that investigates the attitude toward the propositions that speakers/writers express. Features of interest include modal verbs (like 'could'), lexical verbs ('try'), but also nouns ('possibility'), adjectives ('possible') and adverbs ('likely'). The modal systems that are of particular interest in relation to the HT corpus are the *deontic*, concerned with one's 'attitude to the degree of obligation attaching to the performance of certain actions', the *epistemic*, concerned with one's 'confidence or lack of confidence in the truth of an expressed proposition', and the *perception*, also communicated through a degree of commitment to the truth of a proposition, but a degree given specifically by some reference to (mostly visual) perception (Simpson, 1993, p. 47, 48, 50).

Finally, we also analyse some noteworthy images of the manageable, yet representative, set of fifty-three media texts on HT in either its original print or online form multimodally, in an approach consistent with the social semiotic multimodal analytical paradigm, covering aspects relating to the relevant photographs' representational, interactional, and compositional meaning (Kress & Van Leeuwen, 2006). Besides, much like the surrounding verbal text, photographs make a significant contribution to a news story's meaning, and are deserving of the same scrutiny as the verbal text (Caple, 2013, p. 3).

RESULTS

Metaphors

One frequent conceptual mega metaphor is that of TRAFFICKING IS A TRADE. See, for instance, references to people as 'cargo', 'commodities', or 'investment' to be 'bought' and 'sold' in a 'trade', 'market' or 'business'. In '"well stocked" orphanages were seen as a successful business venture', people are conceptualised along the lines of goods with 'worth', or as livestock worth exploiting. This qualitative finding is supported by the

---

[18] As these automated methods cannot account for subtleties and irregularities in the English language, quantitative results are only to be taken as an approximation.

categorisation of key words, as at least 0.5% of corpus tokens[19] have been categorised as Trade-related. Given that at least 0.85% of tokens are categorised as Abuse/Exploitation-related, and 0.63% as Movement-related, the Trade-related percentage is high; Trade is clearly an important semantic category. Wmatrix similarly shows that a full 2.4% of all items in a 100,000-word sample corpus are in the semantic domain of 'Business'. When considering pushed domains, following Koller et al. (2008), this number rises to 3.3%. The majority of key words categorised as Trade-related are to do with acts of trading, such as *buying* and *selling*. This Trade metaphor is clearly grounded in the everyday practices of human traffickers; since trafficking literally involves the illegal trade of people as stock, one may question whether TRAFFICKING IS A TRADE is metaphorical at all.

The following excerpt illustrates the difficulty in distinguishing between the metaphorical and actual trade in human beings:

> Anyone with the slightest degree of worldliness would have thrown the deal back in the Calcutta Wallah's face but, partly through ignorance, partly through short-term greed, and partly because he persuaded himself it might be in the girls' best interests, Chandra signed the contract of indentures. By doing so, he <u>sold</u> his daughters into seven years of slavery and almost certain sexual degradation. (Darbyshire, 2000, emphasis added)

The full article describes how these girls' father, Chandra, in a time of grief and in a very difficult economic position, was persuaded to give up two of his daughters, in exchange for an up-front sum, future monthly payments, and the promise that they would be trained and cared for. This complex situation is then simplistically described as a trade of money for girls.

Regardless of whether this use of TRADE is metaphorical or literal, the press adopting this metaphor invites an acceptance of the ideology whereby people *are* commodities. News texts focusing on the trade-element of trafficking, rather than, for instance, survivors' suffering or how to recognise trafficking, perpetuates the idea that human beings *can* be treated as goods. Though highly conventional (see Kövecses, 2010, p. 211), this mega metaphor still requires a critical response; it contributes to the ongoing objectification of victims/survivors, and to the erasure of HT victims' agency.

---

[19] This is the total number of words in the corpus.

A second cluster of conceptual metaphors revolves around the nature of trafficking and how to respond to it. TRAFFICKING is frequently conceptualised as A SPREADING UNWANTED SUBSTANCE and as one which CAN BE BROKEN, and indeed common responses to trafficking are in line with the metaphor RESPONDING TO TRAFFICKING IS WAR. These metaphors are related in the sense that the representation of trafficking as a threatening physical matter creates a matter that can physically be fought. They also oversimplify responding mechanisms and suggest that HT is something to deal with in a reactionary rather than preventative manner.

The TRAFFICKING IS A SPREADING UNWANTED SUBSTANCE metaphor is found in references to trafficking as 'epidemic', 'widespread', or 'rampant'. What spreads seems to be both the victims and the perpetrators of this crime; there is an 'influx' of those prone to trafficking 'pour[ing]' into the UK, all the while trafficking 'parasites' need to be 'curb[ed]' or 'root[ed] out'. The overwhelming and indeed growing matter of trafficking is emphasised throughout the corpus. Of collocates to *trafficking*, 14.56% indicate either growth (*more, rise*) or imply largeness (*most, scale*). Wmatrix shows that 0.37% of items in the Wmatrix sample corpus are tagged N3.2+, indicating largeness and growth. Furthermore, numbers, such as *billion, millions, thousands,* and *hundreds* form another 1.69% of the Wmatrix sample corpus. These words can refer to numbers of victims as well as profits made through trafficking, but nonetheless underscore the scale of this problem.

The metaphor TRAFFICKING IS A SUBSTANCE which CAN BE BROKEN is found in references to 'strong' units to 'crackdown', 'break up', 'rap', 'stamp out', 'smash', or 'crush' the gangs or HT problem. RESPONDING TO TRAFFICKING IS WAR is found in the texts' reference to a need for an 'international onslaught' to 'tackle', 'combat', 'fight', 'target', 'confront', 'attack', 'purge' or 'spearhead' against trafficking. See, for instance, discussions of 'Britain defeat[ing] the slave trade in the nineteenth century [...] by striking directly at the traffickers'. As indicated by the section on Topics, Responses to Trafficking are mentioned throughout newspaper reporting. A substantial number of these Responses are indeed Fight- or War-related. At 0.26% of all tokens, Fight-related Responses are not quite as conventional as Trade-metaphors, but nonetheless noteworthy. Furthermore, 13.40% of collocates associated with *trafficking* indicate Fight-related Responses, compared to 19.14% Legal Process-related Responses. In fact, in the Wmatrix sample corpus, 0.15% of all items are tagged G3, 'War', which rises to a full 1.19% when considering G3 as a pushed domain.

We most often conceptualise war as a violent conflict that engages societies as large as nations. Though the War metaphor suggests there being different sides, who features on each is unclear/hidden. War-related references also problematically conceptualise trafficking as an issue specific nations cause and other nations have to deal with, when the realities of trafficking suggest otherwise. Even more so, metaphorical constructions, such as the one that refers to a telephone hotline as 'the latest weapon in the fight against human trafficking', portray responses to trafficking as a battle against an overwhelming matter, and allow state actors to portray themselves as saviours, with survivors as acted upon, in other words, saved. Such references to trafficking also establish links between trafficking, on the one hand, and masculinity, power and violence on the other. Violence, such metaphorical constructions suggest, legitimises police *violent* reactions to HT, not to mention reducing HT victims to war collateral damage. By focusing on the Fight, survivors' responses to trafficking are, lastly, limited. They are either 'useful' in this fight, by contributing statements and evidence, or they are not. This limitation on options further erases survivors' agency and can actually contribute to their secondary victimisation. Not unlike the notoriously flawed War on Drugs, the trafficking media metaphors fail to focus on structural factors, and instead only respond to symptoms.

Less prominent and hence micro metaphorical spike sample corpus excerpts draw on various other source domains. These include the TRAFFICKING IS DRAMA/SPECTACLE metaphor[20] ('Children forced into Oliver twist thieving', 'Oliver Twist Scenarios happening in our streets and cities', a trafficking case 'could have ended in tragedy', a raid is 'dramatic'); indeed, in the Wmatrix sample corpus, the semantic domain K4, 'drama, the theatre', has a relative frequency of 0.15%. This rises to 0.41% when K4 is a pushed domain. Another is the TRAFFICKING IS HIDDEN/NOT VISIBLE metaphor ('turned a blind eye to trafficking', 'A report entitled Young Invisible Slaves', 'They are effectively invisible, isolated behind the closed doors of private households'), the related semantic domain, A10 ('hiding, showing') making up 0.54% of items in the Wmatrix sample

---

[20] Exploring the gender and age dimensions of this metaphor would be interesting tasks in themselves. Are women and children victims more prone to be referred to via drama metaphors compared to men? Are men more prone to animal metaphors, perhaps? Such questions merit investigation through the use of concordances of Wmatrix examples, though doing so is beyond the scope of the present chapter.

corpus, 1.23% as a pushed domain. A final metaphor, the TRAFFICKING IS ANIMATED AND BEASTLY ('Halt this evil trade', 'we all thought that [slavery] was gone and in the past, but actually it's alive and kicking in London', 'the trade's dark underbelly', 'Sex trafficker known as The Snake') and, in Pope Francis' terms, even VAMPIRIC metaphor ('Bloodsucker [trafficking] bosses', '[l]iving on the blood of the people'), is less clearly present in the Wmatrix sample corpus, as there are no directly corresponding semantic tags. Related tags, however, include L1+ ('alive'), L2 ('animals'), and S9 ('religion and the supernatural'), which occur at relative frequencies of respectively 0.12%, 0.38%, and 0.36%. Note, however, that the first semantic domain, L1+, also includes instances in which someone is literally alive after life-threatening events, and the use of 'life' to indicate someone's daily routines and habits, whilst the last, S9, also includes many instances in which someone's religion is identified. Though each of these metaphors is not prominent individually in the sample corpora, this micro metaphorical set can altogether be read along the lines of the TRAFFICKING IS HORROR STORY metaphor, which itself suggests an audience in need of entertainment of something mysterious, disturbing and fictional. By relating the problem to narratives of horror, stories with binary portrayals of goodness and badness, it is, once, again, simplified.

Metaphorical portrayals of trafficking signal state actors as heroes and reduce victims to the measure of value/usefulness; as such, the media trafficking metaphors prove ultimately unhelpful in responding to the HT problem.

Naming and Describing HT

HT tends to be described as a large, imported, serious problem, which must be responded to urgently. People's suffering tends to be foregrounded, as the section on 'Agency and Focus' also shows, and this suffering is made particularly salient through the use of (negative) sensory-related words.

Spike sample corpus descriptors refer to HT as a sometimes *neutral* 'phenomenon' ('institution', 'state of affairs', 'issue', 'practice', 'area', 'experience') that is *present-day* ('modern day'/'twenty-first century'), *far-reaching* ('global'), even 'necessary'. It's 'really *big*' and *hard to respond to* ('very complicated', 'challenging and complex'), '*organised*' ('operation', 'networks', 'cartels', 'syndicates', 'gang'), and '*a very lucrative business*' ('form of commerce', 'trade', 'market', 'auctions'). It is *low-skill migrant work-related* ('labour', 'employers', 'work(ers)', 'low-skilled migrants'), *morally 'wrong'* ('scandal', 'problem', 'exploitation', 'abuse', 'bad', 'mis/maltreatment', 'vice', 'unfair', 'terrible', 'sham'), *'en/forced'*, *'cheap'* ('low/poverty pay', 'expendable commodities') and involves *'enslavement'* ('slavery', 'servitude', 'handlers'). It is also *criminal* ('fraudsters', 'assault', 'crime', 'offence', 'criminal operations', 'criminality', 'guilty', 'violence'), often *'sex/ual'* ('prostitution', 'rape'), *hidden* ('invisible', 'isolated', 'domestic'), *unsightly* ('monstrous', 'monsters', 'spectacle', 'gruesome'), *'cruel'* ('the evil', 'nastiest', 'barbaric', 'ordeal', 'suffering', 'wicked', 'snared', 'sordid', 'trap'), *'terrible'* ('vile', 'despicable', 'appalling', 'sordid'), *vomit-inducing* ('revulsion', 'disgusting') and *miserable* ('dreadful', 'vulnerability,' and 'misery').

Quantitative results are largely similar, as shown in Table 2.4, in which we categorise c-collocates to *human trafficking*:

C-collocates categorised as 'other' (articles, pronouns, verbs such as 'said' and 'make'), 61% of all c-collocates to *trafficking*, have been excluded from this table. The percentages in this table represent the share each category has of the remaining c-collocates. Certain categories are newly introduced or replace others compared to the categories found through the qualitative analysis. These include 'foreign', replacing 'migrant', which includes words like 'migrant' as well as 'Europe' and 'Britain', indicating trafficking to be an imported issue. New categories relate to those involved, 'people' and 'responders', including words such as 'woman' and 'police'. Other new categories relate to official responses, categorised as either 'fight' ('crackdown') or 'law', indicating legal responses ('court', 'evidence').

Overall, some terms and descriptors vary from neutral, suggesting that there is no problem whatsoever (at least not when looking at them in isolation), to those that, like the metaphor-related analysis showed, relate to a business or trade, to those that suggest there is something wrong (but not necessarily criminal), to those that suggest there is indeed something criminal going on and to those that strongly negatively (and metaphorically) evaluate the issue. The fact that some of these are perception (sight- and taste-) related is interesting. And as the quantitative analysis also suggests, most characterisations of trafficking mark it as a large, modern, imported problem, which is very bad and must be fought. Much like the horror-related metaphor previously touched on, these findings support O'Connell Davidson's (2010) argument as to the modern slavery narrative being fairy-tale-like; a narrative of innocence and evil, its figures problematically 'stripped of ambivalence'.

Table 2.4   Categorisation of c-collocates to 'trafficking'

Category	Frequency	Percentage
Foreign	80,323	17.66
Big	66,312	14.58
Present-day	39,578	8.70
Criminal	39,123	8.60
Number	37,759	8.30
People	31,034	6.82
Fight	27,577	6.06
Organised	21,012	4.62
Neutral	16,640	3.66
Law	15,736	3.46
Lucrative	14,763	3.25
Responder	13,362	2.94
Enslavement	8,299	1.82
Wrong	6,905	1.52
Work	15,811	3.48
Youth	5,378	1.18
Cruel	4,949	1.09
Sexual	4,232	0.93
Hidden	3,774	0.83
Forced	2,263	0.50
Other	710,003	
Total	*1,164,833*	
Total without 'Other'	*444,830*	

Trafficking and Smuggling

As earlier research shows, trafficking and smuggling are, to a certain extent, conflated. An example of this conflation is found in *The Daily Mail*: '[NCIS director general Abbott] said the smuggled immigrants were often victims misled by traffickers about conditions [in Britain]' (Hinckley, 2000). In line with such research, an examination of our spike sample corpus also reveals a close correlation, even conflation, between (potentially illegal) immigration/smuggling and trafficking. See, for instance references to 'a crackdown on people traffickers [following the Home Secretary's promise to] crack down on illegal immigrants', to '[t]raffickers hid[ing] among migrants', to Cameron wanting to 'disrupt the trafficking and smuggling gangs', and to the London Olympics as a 'magnet for people traffickers smuggling sex slaves and illegal workers into Britain'. Similarly, the press reports a man confessing to 'trying to have his son smuggled' while being 'arrested on suspicion of human trafficking', and another mentions '[t]he role of Thai officials in human trafficking [having] been highlighted in a new report. [Thailand] is on the list of worst people-smuggling centres in the world'. Such fusions are particularly problematic in reference to the tabloids' reporting of the migrant crisis of 2015. The article headlined 'The Sun says Evil Traffickers' opens with reference to '[t]he real villains of the migrant crisis [being] the people smugglers'. *The Sun* elsewhere adds that '[m]ilitary strikes against people traffickers causing the Mediterranean migrant crisis could begin in weeks'. These two examples respectively suggest that smuggling/trafficking resulted from, and also caused, the migrant crisis, rather than acknowledging the conditions leading to these migrants' vulnerability in the first place. Elsewhere, a *Sun* headline refers to the Special Boat Service 'trail[ing] traffickers', the article's opening sentence referring to Britain's special forces 'being sent to blow up death-trap ships used by people smugglers', with no sympathy for the predicament those in the boats are in. Lastly, one 2001 *Independent* article even conflates trafficking with not only smuggling but also, additionally, asylum-seeking: 'The number of people being smuggled into Britain [...] has been cut [...] [P]enalties of £2000 per illegal entrant had reduced human trafficking at Channel ports [...] [A]sylum seekers [resort] to desperate measures to gain access to Britain'.

Similarly, as Table 2.5 shows, *smuggling* is used in almost the exact same way as *trafficking* in the wider corpus, with three exceptions; 'routes', 'immigrants' and, perhaps most surprisingly, 'traffickers', are not c-collocates to *trafficking*.

When considering the c-collocates to keywords categorised as 'participants', a similar picture is drawn. The majority of participants with either 'trafficked' or 'smuggled' as a c-collocate are described as having been *trafficked*. Intriguingly, this also includes 'immigrants' and 'workers'. Only 'women' and 'people' are consistently described as having been smuggled, which is contrary to Musto's (2009) and Shalit, Heynen, and Van der Meulen's (2014) findings showing that men are generally represented as having been smuggled, whereas women are normally considered having been trafficked. An optimistic interpretation of the use of these descriptors would be that newspaper writers recognise the scope for exploitation in economic migration, and are offering these people the 'trafficking-victimhood' status in order to make sure they receive assistance and support. However, given the rhetoric of tabloids like *The Daily Mail* and *The Sun*,

Table 2.5 Categorisation of c-collocates of *trafficking* and *smuggling*, with over-lapping words in italics

Categories	Trafficking c-collocates	Smuggling c-collocates
Abuse	Abuse, exploitation, forced, labour, sex, sexual, slavery, violence, work	
Age	Young	
Commodity	Arms, *cocaine*, *drug*, *drugs*, *heroin*	*Cocaine, drug, drugs, heroin*
Communication	*Said*, say, says, told	*Said*
Deviance	Corruption, fraud, *illegal*, laundering, offences, pornography, problem, prostitution, terrorism, *crime*, crimes, *criminal*	*Crime, criminal, illegal*
Geography	*Britain*, British, centre, countries, country, eastern, *Europe*, European, foreign, home, *international*, Ireland, London, national, UK, USA, world	*Britain, Europe, international*
Morality	*Evil*	
Movement	Immigration, smuggling, *trafficking*	*Trafficking*, routes
Number	Many, more, most, rise, scale, number, one, some, three, *two*	*Two*
Participants	Beings, child, children, criminals, *gang*, *gangs*, girls, government, group, *human*, man, men, network, networks, office, officers, organisations, *people*, *police*, *ring*, rings, slave, unit, victim, victims, women, workers	*Gang, gangs, human,* immigrants, *people, police,* traffickers, *ring*
Response	Charged, charges, combat, combating, control, crackdown, face, fight, *operation*, operations, stop, tackle, tackling, accused, alleged, arrested, case, cases, convicted, court, evidence, investigating, investigation, *jailed*, law, laws, legislation, suspected, suspicion, anti, dealing, help, issue, report	*Jailed, operation*
Status	New, *organised*, serious	*Organised*
Time	Now, time, year, *years*, yesterday	*Years*
Trade	*Trade*, business, industry, *money*	*Money, trade*

this seems an unlikely interpretation. For instance, in an article in *The Daily Mail* about NCIS warnings about the trafficking and smuggling of people into the UK, the following, only tenuously related, was added:

> Asylum seekers are putting overwhelming strain on some GPs' surgeries, doctors complained yesterday. Practices in Gateshead said they are having to

organise extra care without extra resources after the arrival of 600 asylum seekers. And a practice in Leicester has threatened to close its list after 430 asylum seekers were moved into its catchment area. (Hinckley, 2000)

One explanation for this discrepancy is that newspapers do not refer to cases of smuggling and trafficking following legal definitions, but instead use *trafficking* as simply the weightier, more loaded term. The loaded *trafficking*, to refer to all movement of people into the UK, is instead used to communicate newspapers' ideology that economic migration is a very serious problem; *trafficking* evidently has more serious connotations than the more accurate but less sensational *smuggling*.

Description of Victims/Survivors

Victims tend to be described in a stereotypical way: as female, young, and coerced, creating an ideal victim.

In the sample of articles that were qualitatively analysed, survivors are mostly unnamed but, when named ('Ms Lin'), tend to be first named ('Abou', 'Anna', 'Favor', 'Han'), which creates a close, intimate relationship with them as opposed to a distant/official one. The spike sample corpus also refers to HT victims being numerous. There is very much a focus on their high volume with either reference to them in terms of groups of a specific number ('eleven', 'thirty', 'fifty-eight') or indeed large numbers ('dozens', 'hundreds', 'thousands', 'million'). The fact that victims are generally perceived as numerous is tied with the notion of trafficking as a large, and growing, problem. In fact, Dijk (2013) notes that the Polish legislature debated whether HT necessarily involved a plurality of victims, as the Polish translation of this phrase, 'handel ludźmi', refers to people as plural. Of the full corpus key words referring to victims, 65.58% are indeed plural (e.g., *girls*). This multitude of victims is also evident in concordance lines, which show results such as '[t]he International Labour Organisation estimates that 20.9 million people are victims of forced labour globally, including victims of human trafficking for sexual exploitation. "While it is not known how many of these victims were trafficked, the estimate implies that there are millions of trafficking victims in the world," said Mr Fedotov' (*The Morning Star*, 2013).

Qualitative analysis of the spike sample corpus also shows that victims are foreign ('mostly from eastern Europe but also Africa, Asia and south America'), 'poor' ('from poor country communities'), 'illegal' ('uncertain legal status'), 'low-skilled' 'jobseekers' ('promised them a job in the UK') or 'labourers' ('workers', 'cheap and expendable labour', 'manicurists'). Most are 'adult', with a focus on those who are female ('women') and young ('youngsters', 'underage', '40 children, including babies'), or both ('young women', '[t]he youngest known girl victim was just 14', 'little girls crying for their mothers').

Several of the key words applied to victims throughout the full corpus indeed indicate a non-British origin: these are *immigrant, migrant,* and *refugee.* Other victims, too, are often identified as non-British: 26% of c-collocates indicating nationality or origin of victim keywords refer to Britain (e.g. *British, London, here*), whereas 58% indicate a non-British location, most often *Eastern Europe* and *Africa.* These c-collocates also include words such as *illegal, across,* and *foreign,* and support the notion that trafficking is framed as an 'imported' problem (see Johnston, Friedman, & Sobel, 2015). It should also be noted that *immigrants, migrants, refugees,* and *workers* are often young (57% of age-related c-collocates), and *workers* are explicitly identified as *vulnerable.* One possible interpretation is that these modifiers are used to negotiate the negative evaluation of migrants in general by British newspapers (see Gabrielatos & Baker, 2008) and the fact that these people may be considered victims of trafficking. However, as the qualitative analysis shows, British newspapers can nonetheless be ruthless about these victims.

The corpus linguistic findings also refer to victims as female. Of the keywords that are used to refer to victims of trafficking and that inherently indicate gender, 60% are female (e.g., *girls, daughter, woman*). Having said that, those victim-labelling related keywords that do not inherently indicate gender (e.g., *victim*) have 54% masculine gender-related c-collocates, a result that can be explained by the fact that gender collocates can indicate deviations from a perceived norm, in the sense that 'lady doctor' and 'male nurse' indicate that doctors and nurses are expected to be respectively male and female. If the majority of c-collocates indicate masculinity, it is possible that survivors are inherently presumed female and their occasional male-ness is noteworthy.

Another *trafficking* finding from the qualitative analysis is that victims are young. The quantitative analysis supports this finding: 24.58% of all key words applied to victims in the full corpus inherently indicate youth (e.g., *girl, boy, baby, children*) while, for the remaining three-quarters of key words that do not inherently indicate youth, 46% of gender-related c-collocates imply youth (e.g., *young, teenage*). A further 29% of age-related c-collocates are generic indicators of age, and even those c-collocates that appear to imply a lack of youth (e.g., *old*) may also be taken as generic, as in the phrase 'X years old'. Concordances show that this is, in fact, how *old* is to be interpreted. According to concordances, victims are generally under the age of twenty-five, although more so in the case of those trafficked for sexual exploitation than those trafficked for labour exploitation. One notable exception is the case of Elizabeth Fritzl, who was forty-two at the time of her release (see for instance Hall, 2009; Milmo & Peachey, 2013; Nicks, 2008; *The Mirror*, 2008).

According to the qualitative analysis of spike sample corpus data, HT victims tend to be sexualised (females are 'forced to prostitute themselves'/'forced into sex work', or referred to as 'sex slaves', 'sex abuse victims') and defined by their vulnerability ('mental disorder', 'disability', 'in trouble', 'fleeing', 'no protection', 'patient', 'undocumented', 'stranded', 'wretched', 'damaged', 'desperate', 'survivor', 'lone mothers', 'boys in their care', 'separated from their families, exposed to hazards and illnesses or left alone on city streets', 'rescued', 'flimsy boats', 'protection', 'starving', 'have to eat air') and captivity ('captive', 'held', '(virtual) prisoners', 'indentured', 'escaped'). They are hidden ('domestic', 'invisible' and 'isolated'), enslaved ('virtual slaves', 'child slaves', 'life of servitude'), violently acted upon ('forced', 'abuse victims') or even referred to as inanimate, things, 'commod[ities]' ('worth less than a shoe', 'cargo', 'cheap and expendable', 'ripe victims'). Those articles referring to specific trafficking cases often do not specify why victims were trafficked and who was behind the operation, a matter we return to shortly in the 'Agency and Focus' section.

These results are unsurprising given that the stereotypical victim of HT is, as noted in this collection's introduction, *female, young, unwilling to perform the work she is doing, but coerced,* portrayals not just common in news media and pop culture, but also shared by policy makers and the public (Buckley, 2009; Dando, Walsh, & Brierley, 2016; Gould, 2010; Musto, 2009). In short, victims of HT are often described in line with Christie's (1986) theory of the ideal victim; she is young and she is female. Furthermore, in line with the representation of HT as a large and growing problem, victims are represented as numerous. Finally, in accordance with the idea that HT is an imported problem and a threat to national security, victims are described as foreign. The stereotypical victim of trafficking is therefore perhaps best described in the following excerpt from *The Daily Mail*: '[a]ccording to information given by the traffickers, many of the victims smuggled into Britain are "vulnerable" young women from poor or broken families' (Borland, 2009).

Description of Traffickers and Related HT-Perpetrators

Traffickers and other perpetrators are less clearly defined. Newspapers appear to focus on victims and their suffering, neglecting to discuss traffickers in depth.

Traffickers are sometimes identified as 'families forced to sell their children to survive' ('Romanian Fana Moses, 32, had given birth and sold the boy' to a 'French' 'childless couple'), but mostly as 'recruitment agencies solely for overseas workers', 'firms', 'businesses', 'traders', 'businessmen looking for cheap and expendable labour', 'salon' owners, 'employers who exploit migrant workers and pay less than the minimum wage', and 'gangs who sell false dreams and trade on the free borders within the EU'. They are 'masters', 'owners', 'captors', 'abusers', and 'slavers of our day'; in other words, they are defined by their ownership of the victims they have 'control and power over'.

They are a 'vice ring': organised, powerful, and criminal, described as 'jungle'/'human'/'people'/'sex'/'Med' 'traffickers', 'trafficking syndicates', 'operations', 'criminal' 'gangs' or 'elements', 'thugs' and also as 'very powerful' 'masterminds', 'politicians and other Establishment/government' 'figures'/'officials' or 'paedophile rings', selling unwilling victims to 'sex' buyers/'clients'/'young' and 'unknown men'. Those transporting the victims are 'haulier', 'lorry'/'van' drivers.

Quantitative analysis also suggests that, like victims, traffickers are numerous. In fact, traffickers are more often plural than victims (at 69.32% compared to 58%). This use of plurals may help to signify the 'large threat' of trafficking, justifying Fight-responses and newspapers' ongoing attention to migration/trafficking. The use of this strategy is illustrated by the following quote from *The Daily Express*, discussing migrants choosing to camp at Zeebrugge rather than Calais: 'Belgian authorities have stopped 890 migrants without residency papers since January—450 of whom travelled to Zeebrugge which is seven miles from Bruges. *Dozens of traffickers* have also been detained' (Sykes, 2016, emphasis added). This excerpt also displays a conflation of trafficking and smuggling, as it is unclear whether these supposed traffickers simply worked to transport people across borders, or did so with the intent of exploiting them.

In the sample corpora, traffickers' foreign nationality is often highlighted ('four Libyans and one Tunisian', 'ten other Hungarians', 'Ivorian', 'Dutchman') or indicated merely by their full, and most often foreign, name ('Wei Yu—a naturalised Irish citizen who lives in Limerick'; 'Razvan

Ursu'; 'Zoltan Raffael'; 'Toi Van Le', and 'Perry Wacker', who was actually smuggling rather than trafficking immigrants into the UK) or surname ('Blaga'), the latter suggesting formality and also distance. Indeed, only 26% of c-collocates referring to nationality or origin to keywords identifying traffickers refer to Britain. This is equal to the proportion of 'local' c-collocates associated with victims. 58% of c-collocates referring to nationality or origin indicates that traffickers are associated with other countries or are *foreign*. This is also similar to the proportion of 'foreign' c-collocates associated with victims. This finding again underlines the interpretation that trafficking is framed as an imported problem. Reporting on the rise in prostitution, for instance, *The Daily Star* claims: 'Large numbers of women are also being trafficked by foreign gangs into prostitution' (Malley, 2006).

Other than these, however, there are few characteristics that traffickers have in common. They include *gangs*, family members (*father, mother*), *men* and *women*. However, most traffickers in the spike sample corpus data are indeed male ('four men', '42-year-old man'), some are female (a 'Nigerian woman', a '19/38-year-old woman'), with their age ranging from nineteen to fifty-seven when specified. In terms of their evaluation, such individuals are 'dubious' and 'unscrupulous' at best, and '(true) bloodsucker bosses', 'callous', 'evil', 'brutal', and 'heartless' 'monsters'/'parasites'/'villains' at worst.

In short, it is difficult to establish whether newspapers actually create a 'big, bad' trafficker, as the characteristics of the represented individuals actually vary. Likewise, in her 6-month corpus containing 354 trafficking cases in news texts, Denton (2010) found that all possible gender- and role-combinations were present. Sobel (2016) also found that while victims are primarily presented as female, traffickers are either mixed, or with their gender unmentioned, something that, for Sobel, is indicative of the gender of traffickers being male, by default. Instead, newspapers appear to focus on the experiences and characteristics of victims. By doing so, they fail to address the structural factors that cause people be involved in trafficking, either as victims or as traffickers.

Agency and Focus

This section argues that there is a general obscuring of agency in acts of trafficking. Furthermore, victims are presented as having little agency. As 5.39% of keywords relate to an act of trafficking and/or abuse, this overall lack of agency suggests that newspapers tend to focus on the suffering of victims, rather than on those parties who cause such suffering in the first place. Having said that, traffickers are generally identified as actors and agents; they are not acted upon either.

This focus on suffering, that does not specify who caused this suffering, is clear when considering the form of those keywords categorised as 'acts of trafficking and abuse'. They are generally nouns (*abuse, death, exploitation, issue, labour, marriage, prostitution, sex, slavery, threat, violence*), intransitive verbs (*died, worked*), or adjectives relating to these nouns (*hard* labour, *modern* slavery, *sexual* exploitation, *sexual* violence). Those transitive verbs that have been included (*forced, trafficked, killed*) are all in the past participle form, meaning that they can also be used to form (agentless) passives, in which the focus is on the subject undergoing the act, rather than on the object performing the act (if at all included).

Qualitative analysis of corpus data revealed many nominalisations. Some are found in the reference to 'economic migration having led to "conditions in which [...] enforced labour could occur"'. Here, the active voice is employed; the nominalised *migration* causes conditions that could lead to enforced labour, rather than identifying the global socio-economic and political factors related to migration. Also notice the nominalisation of 'enforced labour', which leaves it up to the reader to determine who forces labour. Similarly, there is 'abuse' ('cocoa farm abuse', 'suffered'/'subjected to (terrible) abuse'), 'exploitation' ('the exploitation of migrant workers'), violence ('subject to threats of violence') and a 'demand for these crimes', again leaving it unclear who performs these acts. Lastly, in '[s]ex trafficking and illegal workers threaten Olympics', illegal workers are presumably victims of trafficking, but are presented as agents of threat, and as something to be dealt with. They are presented as problem-causing individuals that threaten the major institution that is the Olympics. As these workers are illegal, they are simply stripped of their victim-status.

The sample dataset is also full of agentless passives that do not require the agent to be referred to. Vehicles carrying victims are 'destined' and 'being used' with no indication as to who is behind the act. As taken in by deception, victims are 'promised', 'told' lies, 'cruelly snared' and 'duped'. As goods, victims are 'handpicked', 'scooped up', 'taken'/'separated from their families', 'being b(r)ought', 'sent out' to engage in forced criminality, 'delivered', 'sold', 'trafficked' (sometimes conflated with 'smuggled') and 'sent' to live elsewhere. As kept against their will, they are 'kidnapped', 'held hostage', 'locked (up)', 'held', 'tied (up)', 'hidden', 'imprisoned', and 'crammed' into small spaces. They are also vulnerable when 'exposed to hazards and illnesses or left alone on city streets' and come to be 'used', 'groomed', 'exploited', 'coerced', 'mistreated', 'enslaved', 'given no money', 'denied'/'not afforded'/'robbed'/'deprived of' 'legal'/'basic rights' and 'discriminated against'. As violently acted upon, they are 'forced to work [...] not being given food or paid for their work', 'attacked', '(sexually) abused', 'molested', 'raped', 'beaten' and end up 'traumatised', their lives 'ruined'. Victims are 'stranded', cases are sometimes eventually 'uncovered' and the victims 'found'/'discovered' and 'freed'/'rescued'/'taken to a place of safety'. In other words, victims are always 'done to', whether by the perpetrators or the police. They lack agency. As these forms allow the actor to be discarded (Jeffries, 2010), newspapers do indeed appear to focus more on the acts of trafficking and abuse than on those performing these acts.

Some of the keywords in this category have an ambiguous form, that is, it is unclear whether they should be read as adjective, noun, or verb. *Domestic*, for instance, can refer to a person working as a domestic servant, but can also be used to refer to *domestic slavery*. More striking is the set of words that can technically be read either as a noun or a verb. These are *attack, force, murder, rape, work, services, hit*, and *trafficking*. If taken to be verbs, they would mostly be present tense first person ones, a form not commonly used in newspaper writing; the most straightforward interpretation is that these are actually nouns.

When considering the grammar of those target words that specifically refer to traffickers, another pattern emerges. Despite a general lack of focus on traffickers (traffickers are also only explicitly referred to half as much as victims), traffickers are assigned much more agency than victims. They are the grammatical subject more often than victims are, at 39.58% against 31.77%. Victims, on the other hand, are more often the grammatical object. More importantly, traffickers are identified as agents (through the collocating preposition 'by') at 2.46%, against victims' 1.46%. These tendencies are especially pronounced in the target nouns *trafficker* and *victims*. At 7.52%, *trafficker* is particularly often indicated as an agent in passive sentences. Furthermore, a *trafficker* is often the grammatical subject of an active, rather than a passive, sentence.

In other words, nominalisations and transitivity analysis reveal that traffickers act, victims are powerless and acted upon, and victims' suffering remains the focus of these texts. Traffickers' direct responsibility for this suffering lacks exposure.

Modality

This section turns to the attitudinal study of the language used in the spike sample corpus texts specifically. It shows that the use of deontic modality suggests that HT is presented as something that must urgently be dealt with, whereas the use of epistemic modality is used by journalists to overstate the scale of the problem and to present the problem as (excessively) serious, without having to write untruths.

The *deontic* modality system, that of duty, is expressed through verbs like 'should' ('members states should step up', 'The harrowing testimony of a woman forced into sex slavery as a teen in Ireland should be a wake-up call'), 'let' ('Police let them walk away'), 'must' ('We must make sure they are aware there are women held against their will', 'they must prostitute themselves', 'A FIRM deadline must be put in place'), 'need' ('Consumers also need to be aware of potential exploitation of nail bar workers', 'People really need to open their eyes', 'a fuller package of proposals is needed'), 'commit' ('the European Convention on Human trafficking commits signatories to tackling the traffickers'), 'allow' ('In future domestic workers will only be allowed in on non-renewable business visas'; 'freed victims of trafficking will be allowed to stay', 'allowing her to be raped by a string of men', 'allowed employees to be paid appropriately') and 'oblige' ('Britain […] is not obliged to take refugees'). Overall, deontic expressions are very often to do with what victims and potential victims are and are not 'allowed' to do, what 'we'/the politicians/police/states should be doing, and what laws commit/allow people to do things. The news texts suggest that there is urgency, commitment, and necessity to respond to the HT problem.

The *epistemic* system deals with (un)certainty. Certainty is often communicated through the verb 'will' ('[trafficking] will continue to exist'; 'Illegal immigrants will continue to pour into the UK', 'Britain will remain the number one destination for sex-slave traffickers'). Uncertainty, on the other hand, is expressed through verbs like 'may' ('The slave traders may dump [their cargo of children] overboard'; 'Criminals may make promises', 'what may be hundreds of people'), 'can' ('child labour can involve youngsters', '[t]he type of work children can be involved in differs greatly', 'slavery can involve sexual exploitation', 'someone can make £1 million a year out of 10 women'), 'could' ('She could then earn her buyer £800 a day', 'Migrant workers […] could become virtual slaves', 'It could have ended in tragedy/be abused by illegal immigrants'), 'would' ('patrolling the African sea-lanes would be a far wiser policy than […]', 'the convention would help Britain', 'it is just inconceivable they would give evidence to trial', 'They <u>would</u> leave migrant workers [...] destitute and homeless'; 'Changing employers <u>would</u> not be appropriate', 'Home office policy reversal <u>would</u> strip them of their right [...]') and 'might' ('<u>might</u> have been involved in the human trafficking syndicates', '<u>might</u> have become a watery grave'). This first set of epistemic phrases presents human trafficking as a very serious, large, problem, without the journalist having to present precise numbers. This also allows them to increase the threshold value (see Galtung & Ruge, 1965) of this news.

Uncertainty is also communicated through nouns ('a <u>possibility</u> for sexual exploitation', '<u>allegations</u> that they treat their workers [... like] slaves'), adjectives ('<u>possible/alleged</u> victim/abuse/people trafficking', '<u>suspected</u> traffickers/victims of human trafficking'), and adverbs like 'allegedly' ('<u>allegedly</u> held as slaves') and 'likely' ('Gangs are <u>likely</u> to target', 'the migrant crisis was <u>likely</u> to make people-trafficking globally easier', 'more <u>likely</u> to be in unpaid family work'). Such uncertainty is also expressed through (visual) perception modality ('If you see a car wash, and it is <u>clear that people look like</u> potentially being exploited', 'workers <u>look</u> hungry', 'who doesn't <u>look like</u> he works in that world', '<u>clearly</u> the problem is most serious in lower income countries', 'she <u>seemed</u> uncertain'). Uncertainty can also be communicated through cognition modality, that is, uncertainty through belief ('officers <u>believe</u> women are frequently raped', 'cages <u>believed</u> to have been used'). As epistemically modalised expressions allow the writer to say things that might not be true and are often (legally) necessary, their overuse exaggerates the nature/extent of the problem, again increasing threshold value, and can even generate panic.

Speech and Writing Presentation

This section turns to the voices behind such urgency and uncertainty. Other than the reporting voice, who/what else is quoted? It shows that primarily powerful people are quoted. This is problematic, as by reporting certain opinions over others, reporters lend legitimacy to these viewpoints over others (Louw, 2005). This may not be intentional, but journalists often report the viewpoints of people who are perceived as authoritative sources, who also tend to be socially powerful (Cottle, 2003; Kuhn, 2007; Machin & Niblock, 2006).[21]

---

[21] Two particular matters should also be considered in this regard: news values, and churnalism. News values are those aspects of a story that editors assume spark interest in readers (Bednarek & Caple, 2012, p. 40); stories with those elements tend to be overrepresented

When exploring the spike sample corpus data in terms of who does and does not talk and write, we found that the reported tend to be either police officers (such as Detective Superintendents, Deputy Chiefs and Inspectors), and also various senior government members and ministers. The latter range from the Prime Minister (or their spokesperson/advisor), the (Shadow) Home Secretary, various (foreign office/immigration/ defence) ministers, Home office/UN reports, chief council executives, party (candidate) leaders/(European) Parliament Members, advisers to the parliamentary committee on HT, the anti-slavery commissioner, and even the Governor of New York. Also reported are those parties whose interests lie in protecting victims (including the Pope, judges, community support workers, charity/Union spokespeople, International Labour Organisation specialists/data, 'Save the Children', European Commission reports/working documents), with little said by those parties whose interests lie in protecting those accused of HT (there is just one instance of 'their lawyer said').

Readers also hear nothing from the HT perpetrators and very little from the HT victims themselves (quotes attributed to 'the boy' found in a suitcase and 'a child sex abuse victim' reporting on a UK intranational

compared to stories without. Incidentally, many news values are also those aspects of HT news that are problematically overreported: unambiguity (Galtung & Ruge, 1965)/simplification (Jewkes, 2011), or the binary representation of victims and offenders; sex; violence or conflict; visuals, and the inclusion of/a focus on children (Jewkes, 2011). In other words, problematic representations of HT are perpetuated as they are perceived to resonate with readers, with the result that global inequalities are maintained (Gregoriou & Ras, Chap. 1 in this book). Churnalism is the increasing tendency for journalists to publish any story, 'whether real event or PR artifice, important or trivial, true or false' (Davies, 2008, p. 59). This trend is due to the increased commercialisation of the British press, which led to staff cuts despite growing revenues, and an increased pressure on remaining staff to 'churn out' as many stories as possible, reducing the ability to (fact) check stories and actually do investigative journalism (Davies, 2008). As a result of these pressures, much of modern journalism is little more than the recycling of PR, press office, and wire agency outputs (ibid.). The problem with PR and press offices, however, is that they work for institutions and individuals with their own agenda, such as the police, political parties, the government, and corporations (ibid.). When churnalism and news values are considered together, what becomes clear is that newspapers are given stories that represent events in a way that benefits the establishment— particularly politics and business; have no time to fact check these stories and uncover different perspectives, and are, due to an increasing demand for revenue and readers, pushed to highlight reader-friendly aspects. This becomes more sinister when considering that highlighting these aspects also benefits those organisations whose press offices put out these stories in the first place.

trafficking case are exceptions). In fact, there is reference to the latter being unable to provide necessary evidence altogether ('these women are so traumatised that it is just inconceivable they would give evidence in a trial'). Even though language/communication often proves problematic for victims, and legal consequences may arise when victims do away with their anonymity, the tendency is to silence them completely and regardless.

Multimodality

Lastly, we turn to look at those fifty-three texts we were able to trace the facsimiles (45)/online (8) newspaper article versions of, questioning first the placing of the text among others on the page/relevant newspaper, and second the choice and nature of any accompanying images only some of which are printed, or at least made available to us, in colour.

We were able to locate forty-five of the spike sample corpus articles in the form of facsimiles, which enabled an examination of the journalistic context surrounding the HT articles as originally printed, telling as it might be to consider how the relevant stories relate 'to other stories on the page which are also competing for the reader's attention' (Caple, 2013, p. 160). Surrounding texts mostly dealt with people movement in general (smuggling, refugees and asylum seekers, migrants and deportation), politics, finance, national crises, international relations/conflict, crime (including abuse, murder, and fraud), various other unfortunate events (such as scandals, disasters, and suicides) and, lastly, sex and celebrity. None of these HT-related articles appeared on newspaper front pages. On average, these featured around page 15 in each newspaper and were about 269 words long; these articles' placing far into the paper and short length suggests they are not flagged up as of the utmost importance (see Chermak, 1994), however newsworthy they may be.

Only twenty of the spike sample corpus articles located (fourteen facsimiles, and six online) had any accompanying images. Several of these twenty merely contained photographs of the officials reporting or reported, the victims/perpetrators/officers involved in the cases reported, or displayed HT-related means (lorries, boats, a suitcase) or stereotypical circumstantial scenes (cages, houses, farms, stations and camps, and stock images of workplaces such as nail salons and car washes). Most noteworthy in terms of their relatively large size and enactment of temporal relations/provision of narrative progression (see Caple, 2013, p. 177), are pairs/series of images: that depicting a capsized boat of migrants, that of two women being questioned when found 'crammed' in the back of a van by bight-yellowed servicemen (the attire hence emphasising the latter's official role, see Caple, 2013, p. 49), and that with red-circled supposed traffickers 'hiding' in a group of migrants on a Navy ship. Perhaps most striking, however, are those images depicting (ideal victim) children. One pair of shots depicts a child physically seen inside a suitcase (with one of these shots being an airport scanner image); in another, a colourfully dressed isolated child breaks tiles outdoor in Mumbai; in a third, a group of four 'unaccompanied', the caption says) children walk next to a pond in a refugee camp in Greece at dusk, their reflection seen across the water. This last one adopts the 'iterating', 'matching', and 'mirroring' compositional configuration (Caple, 2013, p. 99) and can be read along metaphorical lines—the life of these children can take several forms, and it is up to us (*Guardian*) readers perhaps, to help them find the right one. Similarly, an image accompanying a *Guardian* article of domestic workers depicts two Filipino women wiping a wooden floor on their knees, and hence also adopts the 'iterating' and 'matching' configuration (though not the 'mirroring' one). Unlike all other images in the sample the perspective of which is horizontal, the camera angle is here high, the two participants are photographed from above, and the viewer is hence placed in a dominant position (Caple, 2013, p. 39); the viewing perspective here suggests a master/employer literally looking down on, and hence metaphorically taking advantage of, the women. In one last image, a man, head cropped off the stock image, is shown washing a car, the sky's slightly cloudy blueness suggesting optimism for one's future.

Such HT-related photojournalism depicts mostly groups rather than individuals, which suggests mid/low compositional salience, construes the news values of 'Impact, emphasising the consequences of an event, but also Superlativeness [as in the maximised or intensified aspects of an event]' (Caple, 2013, p. 41) while, even where subjects are seen in isolation or in pairs, there is a distinct lack of focus on actors' faces or emotional responses. Such images being mostly long shot, with actor faces being obscured and facial features mostly indiscernible or with 'neutral and negative facial affect' (Caple, 2013, p. 79), is suggestive of these foreign-looking migrants (possibly involved in trafficking) being a faceless and nameless group, and one hard for the viewer to relate to or sympathise with; the relationship between the viewer and those viewed is impersonal, detached. There are no frontal angles and no direct gaze at, or acknowledgment of, the viewer, no 'demand' (Kress & Van Leeuwen 2006, p. 118) for the viewer to do anything in response to the image. Represented participants are instead in oblique angles, and merely on 'offer' (Kress & Van Leeuwen, 2006, p. 119) for the invisible viewer's contemplation. The depicted actors are shown mostly engaged in what Kress and Van Leeuwen (2006, p. 79) describe as 'Narrative Structure', that is, 'unfolding actions and events, processes of change, transitory spatial arrangements'. Here, actors are working, walking, falling into the sea, or swimming. Though depicted as agents, the image cropping/framing suggests that it is others who are imposing these actions on those depicted, in fact. Where masses of immigrants are seen crammed in a fishing boat, they are passively being carried, with little indication of who the agent of this potentially criminal action is. Similarly, in those few images where the depicted actors are shown as standing or sitting, these individuals are portrayed as waiting for others to make life-altering decisions as to their future. In sum, the images suggest that all those (potential victims) depicted are ultimately all agentless.

Conclusion

Our quantitative and qualitative critical discourse analysis of 2000–2016 British news media reveals a close correlation/conflation between transnational HT and smuggling (concepts also blurred with those of immigration and asylum seeking), which contributes to HT victim criminalisation. Where female, victims are sexualised, which supports the notion of sexual exploitation being over-reported. Both HT perpetrators and victims are seen as numerous, illegal and non-British. Where the victims are young, vulnerable, coerced, agentless, silenced, unrelatable, and offered merely for reflection, perpetrators of the HT problem vary, are not focused on/ identified, and are not acted upon. HT itself is represented as an imported, perhaps exaggerated problem, which is very bad and must be fought, urgently. Such journalism foregrounding official responses is the result of vested interests, while state actors are shown to be heroes, its victims reduced to the measure of mere usefulness or value.

References

Anthony, L. (2015). *ProtAnt* (version 1.2.0). [Software]. Tokyo, Japan: Waseda University. Retrieved from http://www.laurenceanthony.net/

Baker, P., Gabrielatos, C., KhosraviNik, M., Krzyzanowski, M., McEnery, T., & Wodak, R. (2008). A useful methodological synergy? Combining critical discourse analysis and corpus linguistics to examine discourses of refugees and asylum seekers in the UK press. *Discourse and Society, 19*(3), 273–306.

Bartley, L., & Hildago-Tenorio, E. (2015). Constructing perceptions of sexual orientation: A corpus-based critical discourse analysis of transitivity in the Irish press. *Estudios Irlandeses, 10,* 14–34.

Bednarek, M., & Caple, H. (2012). *News discourse.* London: Continuum.

Borland, S. (2009, July 14). Foreign gangs Rob Britain of £40bn a year. *The Daily Mail,* [no pagination].

Buckley, M. (2009). Public opinion in Russia on the politics of human trafficking. *Europe-Asia Studies, 61*(2), 213–248.

Caple, H. (2013). *Photojournalism: A social semiotic approach.* Basingstoke: Palgrave.

Chermak, S. (1994). Crime in the news media. In G. Barak (ed.), *Media, process and the social construction of crime* (pp. 95–129). New York: Garland Publishing.

Christie, N. (1986). The ideal victim. In E. A. Fattah (ed.), *From crime policy to victim policy* (pp. 17–30). Basingstoke: Macmillan.

Cottle, S. (2003). News, public relations and power: Mapping the field. In S. Cottle (ed.), *News, public relations and power* (pp. 3–24). London: Sage.

Dando, C. J., Walsh, D., & Brierley, R. (2016). Perceptions of psychological coercion and human trafficking in the West Midlands of England: Beginning to know the unknown. *PLoS ONE, 11*(5), 1–13.

Darbyshire, N. (2000, December 27). Children who are sent to 'the circus' one of the *Daily Telegraph*'s Christmas Charities is trying to stop young Nepalese girls being enslaves as prostitutes. Neil Darbyshire reports. *The Daily Telegraph,* p. 24.

Davies, N. (2008). *Flat Earth news: An award-winning reporter exposes falsehood, distortion and propaganda in the global media.* London: Chatto and Windus.

Denton, E. (2010). International news coverage of human trafficking arrests and prosecutions: A content analysis. *Women & Criminal Justice, 20*(1–2), 10–26.

Dijk, A. M. (2013). Combating human trafficking in Poland: When victims are lost in translation. *Washington University Global Studies Law Review, 12*(4), 783.

Fairclough, N. (1992). *Discourse and social change.* Cambridge: Polity Press.

Fowler, R., Hodge, B., Kress, G., & Trew, T. (1979). *Language and control.* London: Routledge.

Gabrielatos, C. (2007). Selecting query terms to build a specialised corpus from a restricted-access database. *ICAME Journal, 31,* 5–43.

Gabrielatos, C., & Baker, P. (2008). Fleeing, sneaking, flooding: A corpus analysis of discursive constructions of refugees and asylum seekers in the UK press 1996–2005. *Journal of English Linguistics, 36*(1), 5–38.

Galtung, J., & Ruge, M. (1965). Structuring and selecting news. In S. Cohen & J. Young (eds.), *The manufacture of news: Social problems, deviance and the mass media* (Revised ed., pp. 52–63). London: Constable.

Gould, C. (2010). Moral panic, human trafficking and the 2010 Soccer World Cup. *Agenda, 24*(85), 31–44.

Gregoriou, C., & Paterson, L. L. (2017). 'Reservoir of rage swamps Wall St': The linguistic construction and evaluation of occupy in international print media. *Journal of Language Aggression and Conflict, 5*(1), 58–83.

Hall, A. (2009, March 11). Fritzl women at war... *The Daily Mail*, [no pagination].

Halliday, M. A. K. (1994). *An introduction to functional grammar* (2nd ed.). London: Edward Arnold.

Hinckley, M. (2000, July 6). We're losing war on people smugglers, warns police chief. *The Daily Mail*, p. 15.

Jeffries, L. (2010). *Critical stylistics: The power of English*. Basingstoke: Palgrave Macmillan.

Jewkes, Y. (2011). *Media and crime* (2nd ed.). London: Sage.

Johnston, A., Friedman, B., & Sobel, M. (2015). Framing an emerging issue: How U.S. print and broadcast news media covered sex trafficking, 2008–2012. *Journal of Human Trafficking, 1*(3), 235–254.

Koller, V., Hardie, A., Rayson, P., & Semino, E. (2008). Using a semantic annotation tool for the analysis of metaphor in discourse. *Metaphorik.de, 15*, 141–160.

Kövecses, Z. (2010). Metaphor and culture. *Acta Universitatis Sapientiae, Philologica, 2*(2), 197–220.

Kress, G., & van Leeuwen, T. (2006). *Reading images: The grammar of visual design* (2nd ed.). London: Routledge.

Kuhn, R. (2007). *Politics and the media in Britain*. Basingstoke: Palgrave Macmillan.

Lakoff, G., & Johnson, M. (1980). *Metaphors we live by*. Chicago: University of Chicago Press.

Lee, C. (2016). A corpus-based approach to transitivity analysis at grammatical and conceptual levels: A case study of South Korean newspaper discourse. *International Journal of Corpus Linguistics, 21*(4), 465–498.

Lima-Lopes, R. E. d. (2014). Transitivity in Brazilian Greenpeace's electronic bulletins. *Revista Brasileira de Linguística Aplicada, 14*(2), 413–439.

Louw, P. E. (2005). *The media and political process*. London: Sage.

Machin, D., & Niblock, S. (2006). *News production: Theory and practice*. Abingdon: Routledge.

Malley, P. (2006, December 14). Why young girls still go on game. *The Daily Star*, [no pagination].

Mayr, A., & Machin, D. (2012). *How to do critical discourse analysis*. London: Sage.

Milmo, C., & Peachey, P. (2013). Women escape after 30 years in UK slavery. *The Independent*, p. 5.

Modern Slavery Act 2015. (c.30). London: The Stationery Office.

Musto, J. L. (2009). What's in a name?: Conflations and contradictions in contemporary U.S. discourses of human trafficking. *Women's Studies International Forum, 32*(4), 281–287.

Nicks, G. (2008, May 23). Cellar dad is benefits cheat. *The Daily Star*, [no pagination].

O'Connell Davidson, J. (2010). New slavery, old binaries: Human trafficking and the borders of 'freedom'. *Global Networks, 10*(2), 244–261.

Poole, B. (2010). Commitment and criticality: Fairclough's critical discourse analysis evaluated. *International Journal of Applied Linguistics, 20*(2), 137–155.

Rayson, P. (2009). *Wmatrix* [Software]. Lancaster: Lancaster University Computer Department. Retrieved from http://ucrel.lancs.ac.uk/Wmatrix/

Richardson, J. E. (2007). *Analysing newspapers: An approach from critical discourse analysis*. London: Palgrave.

Rodrigues, A. S., Jr. (2005). An exploratory study of representation of gay characters in a parallel corpus of short stories: A systemic-functional approach. *Cadernos de Tradução, 2*(16), 83–104.

Shalit, A. D., Heynen, R., & Van der Meulen, E. (2014). Human trafficking and media myths: Federal funding, communication strategies, and Canadian anti-trafficking programs. *Canadian Journal of Communication, 39*(3), 385–412.

Simpson, P. (1993). *Language, ideology and point of view*. London: Routledge.

Sinclair, J. (2005). Corpus and text—Basic principles. In M. Wynne (ed.), *Developing linguistic corpora: A guide to good practice* (pp. 1–16). Oxford: Oxbow Books.

Sobel, M. R. (2016). Confronting sex trafficking: Gender depictions in newspaper coverage from the Former Soviet Republics and the Baltic states. *European Journal of Communication, 31*(2), 152–168.

Sykes, S. (2016, February 15). Fears of Belgian 'jungle' as port migrants move in. *The Express*, p. 6.

Tabbert, U. (2015). *Crime and corpus*. Amsterdam: John Benjamins.

The Mirror. (2008, December 31). Cellar dad's girl back in real world, p. 25.

The Morning Star. (2013, February 13). United Nations highlights scale of human trafficking, [no pagination].

United Nations Office on Drugs and Crime. (2016). *United nations convention against transnational organized crime and the protocols thereto*. Retrieved from

the United Nations Office on Drugs and Crime: http://www.unodc.org/
unodc/treaties/CTOC/

Widdowson, H. G. (1995). Discourse analysis: A critical view. *Language and Literature*, 4(3), 157–172.
Widdowson, H. G. (1998). The theory and practice of critical discourse analysis. *Applied Linguistics*, 19(1), 136–151.
Widdowson, H. G. (2004). *Text, context, pretext: Critical issues in discourse analysis*. Oxford: Blackwell Publishing.
Winterdyk, J., Reichel, P., & Perrin, B. (eds.). (2012). *Human trafficking: Exploring the international nature, concerns, and complexities*. Boca Raton: CRC Press.

CHAPTER 3

Not All Human Trafficking is Created Equal: Transnational Human Trafficking in the UK and Serbian News Media Texts— Narratological and Media Studies Approaches

Nina Muždeka

Abstract This chapter investigates the representation of transnational human trafficking in news texts in English and Serbian (published between 2000–2016 and 2003–2016 respectively) by adopting contemporary narrative and media theories. The identified narrative strategies and narrative elements (pertaining to the fabula, story, and text) not only shape the news texts, but also function as a semiotic code through which reality is itself constructed. In both sets of news texts, narratives as forms of representation prioritize particular aspects of human trafficking (e.g., use of official sources), while neglecting and/or completely excluding others (e.g., roots of human trafficking). The chapter draws attention to the logic behind such mechanisms that transform information into meaningful structures and thus influence the shaping of public perception and responses to this crime.

Keywords Human trafficking • Media studies • Narrative • Narratology • Newsworthiness • Serbian news media texts • UK news media texts

N. Muždeka (✉)
University of Novi Sad, Novi Sad, Serbia
e-mail: nina.muzdeka@ff.uns.ac.rs

C. Gregoriou (ed.), *Representations of Transnational Human Trafficking*, https://doi.org/10.1007/978-3-319-78214-0_3

INTRODUCTION

Transnational human trafficking invites debate on the role of the media as a contemporary watchdog and a forum for showcasing diverse viewpoints. To shed light on some of the mechanisms that direct the media approach to representation of human trafficking (henceforth HT), this chapter investigates the representation of HT in UK and Serbian news media, using contemporary narrative and media theories (Bal, 2009; Fulton, 2005; Jahn, 2005; Zelizer & Allan, 2010). In this approach, HT news media texts in both languages are treated as narratives, that is, forms of representation culturally positioned to turn information into meaningful structures and thus to produce diverse meanings within different social and cultural milieus, addressing and affecting target audiences in specific ways. Narrative and media theories place emphasis on the aspects of narrative structure, construction, form, patterns, medium, and the elementary epistemology of knowing the world.

Fulton (2005) defines the relationship between text and its meaning using broadly defined poststructuralism as a theoretical approach. The basic, but often overlooked, tenet, is the fact that *information* (as a non-narrative segment) does not equal *news* (as a narrative construct). A piece of news represents a "deliberately structured story" (Fulton, 2005, p. 219), not the fact or the truth itself (however we choose to define the concepts of "fact" and "truth"). As a deliberately created structure, a news story "translates" the initial information into meaning using narrative strategies, that is, the narrative construction. The aspects of narrative construction are analysed as a semiotic code in which not only news is created, but also so is a much more encompassing and influential structure: our whole sense of reality of the world that surrounds us, as recipients of news. Since this semiotic code contributes to the process of creating public opinion, perception, and agenda, its analysis also allows investigation into the wider ideological implications and socio-political positioning that lies behind the process of constructing and creating news.[1]

Narrative studies and media and communication studies identify similar aspects of narrative construction as crucial for understanding the process of news creation. Media and communication studies define "narrative" as "the organizing structure of a news story that describes in patterned ways the unfolding of public events or issues within the parameters made

---

[1] Bal (2009, p. 35) insists that "narratological analysis inherently serves political or ideological critique" since ideology cannot be isolated from structure.

available by a technological medium" (Zelizer & Allan, 2010, p. 77). As such, any news narrative "offers a fundamental epistemological way of knowing the world, involving sequence, setting, perspective, characterization, tone, and a relationship with the public" and is "differentiated both by its contents—what it says, the story or plot—and its form—how it says, the act of narration" (Zelizer & Allan, 2010, p. 77). Using different terms but essentially the same logic, Johnson-Cartee (2005, p. 159) defines narrative as a fully developed story that includes "characters, scene descriptions, conflicts, actions with motives, [and] resolutions". What provides the structure is the narrative frame, that is, "the basic organization of the structural components used in the story" (Johnson-Cartee, 2005, p. 159). Referring to the narrative frame, other authors in the field used expressions such as "formulaic narrative construction" (Bird & Dardenne, 1988, p. 67) and "structure of expectation" (Tannen, 1993, p. 15). Irrespective of the exact term used, the essence remains the same—what is noticed and identified is the basic schema or the prototype of organization that transforms various separate structural elements into a coherent narrative structure. Following this logic, it can be argued that what is commonly deemed as journalistic objectivity constitutes "sameness in news" ascribed to the application of a particular narrative frame, not mirroring reality (Bird & Dardenne, 1988, p. 67).

Bal (2009, p. 10) defines narrative as a "cultural phenomenon" consisting of three layers: the text (synonymous with "discourse" or "surface telling", see Fulton, 2005, p. 37; cf. Genette, 1988), the story (synonymous with "plot" and "syuzhet", see Bal, 2009), and the fabula ("a series of logically and chronologically related events [...] caused or experienced by actors"—Bal, 2009, pp. 5–9). Within the analysis of a fabula, I examine the elementary choice of events that make the news. The analysis of elements of a story includes the aspects of characters (who participates?)[2] and focalization (who sees the events?).[3] Here I also analyse the social

[2]While Bal (2009, p. 92) analyses participants in the chosen events at both the level of a fabula (as "actors" or "actants", i.e., "abstract units") and the level of a story (where "actors are 'turned into' characters, placed into specific spaces with mutual symbolic and circumstantial relations"), I opted for the analysis of this element at the level of a story only in order to illustrate better their role in the construction of news as stories with a particular agenda to be promoted. Bal's (2009, p. 129) distinction says that "an actor in a fabula is a structural position, while a character is a complex semantic unit".

[3]Bal (2009, pp. 191–192) considers focalization to be "the most important, most penetrating, and most subtle means of manipulation" which should not be marginalized (in favour of content analysis) when analysing newspaper reports for their "hidden ideology".

groups or individuals that are given voice in the text, by showing which of these are marked as prominent, which are placed in the background, and which are completely neglected/excluded. Within the analysis of text and narration, I investigate the structure of news texts in terms of the dissemination of information, as well as levels of narration (including frame/primary and embedded texts). The aim of the analysis of these three layers of narrative structure is to show how these narrative elements are employed regarding their role in turning information into print media discourses that portray transnational HT in UK and Serbian news media texts. Finally, I interpret the ideological positioning that is created as a result of such a narrative construction, showing how particular ideological standpoints are promoted in the news media narratives on HT.

To maintain consistency across the project, the same English language news media text corpus of sixty-seven texts was used for this analysis as in this collection's Chap. 2. For the selection of the Serbian language texts, the most extensive Serbian news media database (EBART) was used, archiving news media output since 2003. EBART archives both broadsheet and tabloid newspaper sources, of national, regional and local coverage, in both Cyrillic and Latin script.[4] The average number of HT-related news texts was thirty-five per month. The core search terms used were direct translations of the search terms used for the English language corpus: human trafficking ("trgovina ljudima", "trafiking"), slavery ("ropstvo"), modern slavery ("savremeno ropstvo", "moderno ropstvo"), trafficking in human beings ("trgovina belim robljem", "trgovina ljudskim bićima", "trgovina ljudima"), forced labour ("prinudni rad", "prisilni rad"), sexual exploitation ("seksualna eksploatacija"), sex trafficking/sexual trafficking ("seks-trafiking", "seks trafiking"), and sex slave ("seksualno ropstvo", "seksualno roblje"). Articles were manually checked to ensure they were related to HT.[5]

---

[4] The corpus included 315 newspaper articles published in 28 different print news media: *Akter, Balkan, Blic, Borba, Danas, Dnevnik, Ekonomist, Ekspres, Glas javnosti, Građanski list, Informer, Kurir, Nacional, Narodne novine, Naše novine, Nedeljni telegraf, NIN, Novi Magazin, Pančevac, Politika, Pravda, Pregled, Press, Srpski nacional, TV novosti, Večernje novosti, Vranjske,* and *Vreme.*

[5] Most notably, this kind of manual checking for relevance was done because of the high frequency of Serbian texts with the key word "trafika", which is a false friend of English "trafficking" (and denotes a newspaper booth or kiosk—a very frequent robbery target and thus a very frequent occurrence in the news).

Fabula: What to Choose for the News?

In the interpretation of news media texts, fabula—as material which is an essential, basic layer of any narrative—is "the answer to the classic journalist's questions" (Who? What? Where? How? When? Why?) (Conboy, 2007, p. 43). Events featured in British and Serbian news texts on HT were categorized as in the following subsections.

Arrests and Reports on Criminal Acts

As the most prominent and numerous articles on HT in both UK and Serbian news print media, these cover the incidents that happened most recently. In the fabula of these texts, two events are typically featured: the act of arrest, and the criminal act perpetrated by the arrested and/or trafficked person/people. The UK press reported on a "Man seized for slavery", the discovery of illegal immigrants found in the back of a lorry, and the arrest of a man after a 26-year old Romanian victim is found by the police (*The People*, 2016; *The Daily Star*, 2016; *The Guardian*, 2015[6]). In Serbian media, similar events occur: the arrest of 13 people found smuggling illegal immigrants in Vranje in June 2015, the arrest of a theme park owner suspected of keeping a slave for 4 years, the arrest of a group suspected of forcing a 16 year old girl into prostitution, and the arrest of a person suspected of selling a girl into forced marriage (*Blic*, 2013b; *Informer*, 2013, 2014; *Večernje novosti*, 2015b).

Court Proceedings

This group includes trials and sentences for HT-related criminal acts. Articles stemming from them also feature at least two events—those related to the court (the trial, witness statements, sentencing), and those referring to the actual HT-related crime (mentioning victims and/or circumstances of the criminal act). The UK press reported on "'Trafficked' Briton to lodge drugs death-sentence appeal" (Fearn, 2015), on the sentence of "14 years for trucker who left 58 to die" (Leonard, 2001), and a sex trafficker "convicted of rape, conspiracy to traffic and conspiracy to control prostitution" (*The Sun*, 2015). Similarly, in the Serbian press, some of the numerous examples

---

[6] Those news articles in which the author's name was not given are referred to by virtue of the publication.

are: a criminal duo sentenced to 5 years in jail for trafficking a 19-year-old girl, a Pakistani man sentenced to 3 years for HT in Serbia, a report from the ongoing trial of a criminal group of 10 people suspected of trafficking a girl (*Danas*, 2004b, 2015; *Večernje novosti*, 2004a) and so on.

Official Reports on HT

These articles usually summarize facts and figures related to HT for a given period and country/region. The reports and studies are issued by authorities and agencies either linked to the government or to NGOs. In the UK press, articles were triggered, for example, by the publication of an EU report on HT and a Home Office report on HT (Rankin, 2016; *The Times*, 2007). The examples from the Serbian press include: a UN report on organized crime in South-East Europe, ASTRA anti-trafficking organization's report for 2010, and a US State Department report on HT (*Blic*, 2004; *Pregled*, 2011; *Večernje novosti*, 2007b).

Planned Responses to HT

These events are found in the announcements from the authorities regarding their plans to respond to HT. The UK press reported, for example, on "UK police [having been] deployed to Calais to tackle people-trafficking gangs" (Smith, 2015), "Britain to send intelligence officers to Sicily to 'disrupt' human traffickers" (Watt, Travis, & Mason, 2015), and the Home Secretary announcing "plans for a crackdown on trafficking gangs" whilst also signing "the European Convention on Human Trafficking which commits signatories to tackling the traffickers and helping victims" (Harrison, 2007). Serbian media similarly published articles headlined "Serbia to decisively fight HT" (*Nedeljni telegraf*, 2008) and "Battle strategy to combat HT" (*Politika*, 2006) (in which government officials expand on the proposed strategies), as well as the article on signing the UN anti-trafficking protocol in 2004 (*Danas*, 2004a).

HT-Related Public Events

These include seminars, round tables, public lectures, film screenings, theatre performances, public campaigns, and similar events related to HT. In UK newspapers, such was the article on the slavery summit held by "Britain's top confectionery companies" (Clark, 2001). Serbian print media featured, for example, a conference on HT in South-East Europe, a round table organized by an OSCE mission to Serbia, the Serbian Department of Justice, and the Victimological Society of Serbia, an anti-HT campaign launched by "Beosupport" (NGO), and a conference held to publicize a Serbian film on HT (*Danas*, 2005; *Glas javnosti*, 2004a; *Politika*, 2004; *Pravda*, 2010).

Personal Experience/Victim Targeting and Victim Profiling

The UK print media wrote as to "Five myths about child labour" (Kweifio-Okai, 2015) to determine whether child labour occurs in rich countries, and about "three women [having been] kept captive for 30 years" in South London (Butler & Bowcott, 2013), revealing both the story of victims' discovery and their position prior to it. Serbian media feature stories about recruiting victims (especially women and children) that both highlight their personal experience and serve as a warning for those prone to being trafficked.

STORY: FRAMING AND MANIPULATING THE FABULA

As the middle of the three layers of the narrative, a story consists of material "not different from that of either the text or the fabula", but "looked at from a certain, specific angle" (Bal, 2009, p. 91). To create the story, the fabula is "treated" and manipulated through inscription of a particular ideology (Bal, 2009, p. 92).[7] In HT news texts, this "manipulation" of the fabula most notably takes form through creation/highlighting of news values[8] and focalization. In media studies, such promoting of "issue prioritization" and increasing of "issue accessibility" is referred to as "agenda setting" and "priming" (Johnson-Cartee, 2005, p. 25).[9]

[7] Bal (2009, p. 92) treats "manipulation" and "manipulated"in their original meaning of "handling, treatment, operation".

[8] In media studies, there is the question of the extent to which news values are intrinsic to an event. While Galtung and Ruge (1965, p. 71) maintain that an event "either possesses [news factors] or does not possess them", discursive analysis focuses not on how an event is selected as news, but how it is *constructed* as news (Bednarek & Caple, 2017, p. 43; original emphasis).

[9] Johnson-Cartee (2005, p. 17) identifies three aspects of every mass-communicated news report's influence: agenda setting, priming, and framing. While the first two aspects show how news draw attention to some aspects of the story at the expense of others, framing

Newsworthiness, or How to Make a Story Publishable

For Bal (2009, p. 91), the story is "the result of an ordering". Similarly, ordering or structuring is inherent in the process of creating a news story. In structuring news, the relevant elements of the fabula are tested against their newsworthiness—the list of criteria[10] that contribute to the appeal of the news story to general audiences and deem the news story as one worth publishing. While it is true that various authors use different terms for news values, and that the exact number of identified criteria varies (cf. Brighton & Foy, 2007, pp. 7–11), common factors are: oddity, proximity, timeliness, prominence, consonance, consequence, the number of those affected, negativity, and human interest.

Oddity/Exceptional Quality

As a news value that determines how uncommon the event is, oddity "is about establishing contrast with the expected" (Bednarek & Caple, 2017, p. 66). The British news piece "Women for sale in Gatwick slave auctions" (Taylor, 2007) emphasizes this news value in its very headline. Since this value depends on the target audience and "their experience of the world" (Bednarek & Caple, 2017, p. 66), an event may be construed as exceptional if it does not conform to stereotypes and statistical norms. This is seen in the following Serbian news texts, which translate into: "The greatest victims of HT are—construction workers!", "Proletariat in greater danger than sex workers", "[A] victim is also of masculine gender", "Men increasingly becoming victims of HT", and "Men are slaves too" (*Dnevnik*, 2014; *Naše novine*, 2014; *Politika*, 2009a, 2009b; *Večernje novosti*, 2007a). These texts indicate that the public expects typical victims of HT to be women forced into prostitution; that men (or construction workers/proletariat) are increasingly becoming victims of HT is unexpected.

An exaggerated aspect of this news value is shock value or scandal (cf. Brighton & Foy, 2007, p. 8). This value is obvious in the UK example of

focuses on "how news content affects and influences news consumers" (Johnson-Cartee, 2005, p. 25) and are discussed under "Ideological positioning". For a detailed overview of agenda setting, priming and framing theories, see Johnson-Cartee (2005, pp. 17–31).

[10] Bednarek and Caple (2012, p. 37), citing Bell (1991, pp. 180, 194, 320), refer to news values as both "qualities" and "criteria". For Bell (1991, p. 169), news values lead to "events being framed in a particular way". Analysing the process of creating and structuring news, Galtung and Ruge (1981, p. 60) state that "events become news to the extent they satisfy" the list of "conditions" known as news values.

the Gatwick slave auctions, since the text not only depicts HT as a form of modern-day slavery, but also slavery happening out in the open, in a first-world country. It is also blatantly emphasized in the following examples from Serbian press: "A girl sold for a laptop and €100", "A bride sold for €1000", and "A man sold his pregnant wife for €1500, then reported her kidnapped" (*Blic*, 2013b; *Press*, 2012; *Večernje novosti*, 2015a). Not only do these articles emphasize the unexpected behaviour, but also behaviour that is generally unacceptable according to social norms. By specifying the exact amount of money for which a human being is sold, the texts under-line the shocking aspect of the event.

Proximity

According to Bednarek and Caple (2012, p. 42), what is newsworthy "usually concerns the country, region or city in which the news is pub-lished". In addition to geographical nearness, which extends to include neighbouring countries, proximity also refers to cultural closeness. Hence most news stories on HT published in both UK and Serbian media refer to events that occurred in these countries, or in countries perceived as culturally close to these countries. The UK press, for example, featured a story headlined "Scandal of the 'slaves' who pamper the nails of rich New Yorkers" (Usborne, 2005). The fact that the same sort of situation occurs in UK nail bars "employing" immigrant women also makes the story relevant to a UK audience. There is also a story about a "Baby 'sold' for £6,500 and a BMW" (*The Daily Mail*, 2015), which took place in France, a country geographically close to the UK. In Serbian media, there has also been a marked interest in the events occurring in/linked to the region of ex-Yugoslav countries and the Balkans (Croatia, Bosnia, Montenegro, Kosovo), which all belong to the same HT route. However, placing emphasis on the scandal or shock value is also enough to get a story published even if it happened at distant locations. The UK press featured the story of "A boy smuggled in a suitcase" (Badcock, 2015) tak-ing place at the border between Morocco and the small Spanish territory of Ceuta, North Africa. In Serbian media, the story headlined "Moldova, the country of sex slavery" (*Politika*, 2007) claims that 10% of inhabitants of Moldova are victims of HT, that 400,000 young Moldavian women are victims of sex slavery, and that paedophiles from all over Europe fly in once a week to satisfy their appetites with the government's consent. The range of shocking details is enough to make the story appealing to the Serbian audience, although the factors of geographical and cultural proximity are here missing.

Timeliness

Similarly, events that are recent or "temporally relevant to the reader" (Bednarek & Caple, 2012, p. 42), in line with general journalistic emphasis on a "24 hour news cycle",[11] have precedence. This is especially true for what are known as hard news texts.[12] Most texts published in both UK and Serbian print media feature events that have only just happened (e.g., recent arrests, court hearings, and announcements).

Prominence

News stories that feature celebrities, politicians, or even particular nations (perceived as geographically or culturally close to the relevant readership) are considered newsworthy. This is evident in the example from the UK press headlined "I was trafficked by Westminster abuse ring": "Vulnerable boys were trafficked from a children's home before being abused by *'very powerful' figures* in a Westminster paedophile ring, a victim has claimed. [...] Once in the capital, they were molested by *politicians and other Establishment figures...*" (Marsden, 2015, my emphasis). In Serbian media, a lot of public attention—not only in Serbia but in the whole ex-Yugoslav region—went to a specific case of HT in which the Deputy Public Prosecutor in Montenegro was arrested for trafficking women (see *Danas*, 2004c; *Večernje novosti*, 2004b).

Consonance

Consonance refers to "the extent to which aspects of a story fit in with stereotypes" (Bednarek & Caple, 2012, p. 56) about a nation, region, issue, person, and so on. This news value has been particularly emphasized in Serbian media, where the majority of HT news reports up to 2005 aimed to reinforce the stereotypes of victims being sex-trafficked girls from former Eastern bloc countries and Albanian nationals as traffickers. In British media, texts about foreign traffickers confirm the stereotype that HT is an imported problem caused by particular ethnic groups (e.g., traffickers from Hungary in "Sex trafficker facing prison", *The Sun*, 2015, or Romanian gypsy traffickers in "Baby is 'sold' for £6,500 and a BMW", *The Daily Mail*, 2015).

---

[11] Bednarek and Caple (2012, p. 20) define news cycle as "the time span between the publication/broadcast of a newspaper or news programme and the next edition".

[12] Hard news are "news associated with importance, significance, immediacy and relevance" (Zelizer & Allan, 2010, p. 53), as opposed to soft or human interest news "that are not necessarily specific to a particular day, but provide background or a 'human interest' angle" (Fulton, 2005, p. 226).

Number/Consequence/Impact

Space in the news will be more readily given to those HT stories that include/affect a considerable number of individuals, bear more consequence and have greater impact than others. The UK article "348 held over Canadian child porn" (*The Daily Telegraph*, 2013) tells the readers that "More than 300 people including *teachers and doctors* have been arrested *worldwide* on *child pornography* charges after a Canadian-led investigation" (my emphasis). The newsworthiness is first created through shock, emphasizing the contrast between the publicly perceived trustworthiness of the professions of those arrested, and the criminal activity of child pornography. The fact that the criminal activity was widespread adds to the impact. Although in the following example voluntary migrant movements do not constitute an act of HT per se, the sheer number of people involved is what makes this UK story newsworthy: "Up to *700* migrants and refugees are feared to have drowned in the Mediterranean [...], making it *the deadliest week* this year [...]" (Squires, 2016, my emphasis). The UK article headlined "Domestic workers: 47 million people worldwide denied basic labour rights" (Kelly & Scruton, 2015) also emphasizes the vast number of people affected, while simultaneously underlining the "worldwide" aspect of the case, and hence the universality of its consequence and impact. The following examples from Serbian press similarly emphasize the newsworthy value of "number": "Nearly *200,000* women caught in trafficking network" and "*700,000* people sold around the world each year" (*Danas*, 2003; *Glas javnosti*, 2004b, my emphasis).

Negativity

In journalism, negativity is referred to as "the basic news value" (Bell, 1991, p. 156), since news stories "frequently concern 'bad' happenings" (Bednarek & Caple, 2012, p. 57) such as conflicts, damage, or wars. Construing the value of negativity proved to be easy in HT news stories in both languages since most news texts on HT develop the conflict along the line of criminals vs. the police force/judicial system. In the UK press, such are the articles headlined "Britain to send intelligence officers to Sicily to '*disrupt*' human traffickers" (Watt et al. 2015), and "Reid out to *crush* 21st-century slave trade" (Harrison, 2007). Also, the lead sentence of the article on New York nail bars states that "Andrew Cuomo, the Governor of New York, has ordered a *crackdown* on nail salons" (Usborne, 2005) in which "undocumented immigrant women" are treated as "slaves" (my emphasis). The Serbian press features the following examples: "Serbia to decisively *fight* HT", "*Battle* strategy to *combat* HT", and "*exterminate* modern slavery" (*Kurir*, 2012, my emphasis; *Nedeljni telegraf*, 2008; *Politika*, 2006). The choice of the expressions used heightens the tension created. However, the apparent conflict does not necessarily have to produce a negative effect, since the intended outcome of these actions (stopping criminals/HT) is not negative.

Human Interest

Human interest or personalization is the aspect emphasized in those news stories that "give a human face to the news" (Bednarek & Caple, 2012, p. 44). As such, it is an aspect more common in soft news. See, for example, a UK press article headlined "Persecution and poverty driving the Gypsies of Romania to Britain" (Phillips, 2013). In Serbian media, such an example comes from a text on trafficking of babies in China (*Politika*, 2009d)—although lacking in proximity, the Serbian media still considered this story newsworthy because it presents a deeply touching issue with which the audience can sympathize irrespective of the country in which this audience lives.

Focalization, Characters and Stereotypes

As Bal (2009, p. 161) claims, whenever events are presented, they are presented from a certain point of view, which implies the "subjective nature of story-telling", even in journalism. Instead of "point of view", Bal (2009, p. 162) uses the term "focalization", because it allows her to distinguish between "those who see and those who speak".[13] The analysis of news texts on HT in both languages revealed that most news reports were prompted by noteworthy events, such as court proceedings, arrests, or government policy announcements. These events were commented on by representatives of the government, police, judiciary system, and other official establishments. Given that these commentators function as characters who see, that is, focalizers, focus is placed on the one-sided, "official" point of view. Such focalizers in the UK texts are: "Detective Superintendent Mark Ponting, of the Metropolitan Police", "Commander Sue Wilkinson, also of the Met", "Anti-slavery Commissioner Kevin Hyland", "Mr Justice

---

[13] Bal (2009, p. 162) also acknowledges the following terms used in narrative theory to denote point of view: narrative perspective, narrative situation, narrative viewpoint, and narrative manner.

Alan Moses", "prosecutor Karen Wiseman", "Home Secretary John Reid", "representatives of Scotland Yard", "officials who scanned a suitcase at the border", "the civil guard", and "the Pope" (Badcock, 2015; Leonard, 2001; Taylor, 2007; *The Daily Mail*, 2016; *The Daily Star*, 2008; *The Daily Telegraph*, 2015). As for the Serbian media, the focalizers featured are: the "Minister of Economy Predrag Bubalo", the "Minister of the Interior Ivica Dačić", the "national anti-trafficking coordinator", and the "United States Ambassador to Serbia Mary Warlick" (*Dnevnik*, 2009; *Kurir*, 2012; *Politika*, 2006, 2009c). These characters need not be individualized by their name, because it is their function that bears most relevance. Although both the official perspective and the fact that the news stories were prompted by establishment-related events might signal journalists' intention to provide an objective framework for the interpretation and analysis of the news stories, whether this objectivity is (or indeed, can be)[14] achieved is questionable. Favouring only one perspective signals partiality and the exclusion of alternative perspectives and frameworks of interpretation. My analysis thus contests the claim that, as "an autonomous sphere of social influence, which reports the facts honestly and even-handedly to raise the consciousness of the audience and act as a force for social good" (Stockwell, 1999), news media are placing emphasis on objectivity.

Aside from focalizers, HT-related texts in both languages also feature characters who do not provide perspective. In the above-mentioned UK news texts, such characters are: "children forced into thieving", "youngsters who should be in school", "trafficking gangs", "organized criminals", "women being sold into prostitution", "women openly sold outside a café", "28 illegals", "evil lorry driver Perry Wacker", "illegal Chinese immigrants", "sex slave traffickers", "an eight-year old Ivorian boy", and "a 42-year-old man from Ivory Coast". In Serbian texts, such characters are: "Saša B. from Kačarevo", "Mile M., a theme-park owner from Aleksinac", "a 16-year old girl", and "B.M., a man from Novi Sad" (*Informer*, 2014; *Kurir*, 2013; *Press*, 2012; *Večernje novosti*, 2015a). These individuals are real people who have been turned into characters of a narrative and "attributed with social roles, personal qualities and actual utterances" (Fulton, 2005, p. 237). In the interpretation of a HT news story, they stand as representatives of a social class, gender, or group (such as migrants, illegals, vulnerable women, innocent children, cunning traffickers). This reading

[14] For more on the impossibility of achieving objectivity, see Fulton, 2005, p. 231.

within the suggested social, cultural, or political context produces stereo-typical perception of participants in the HT process.[15]

Stereotyping of characters is especially prominent in those Serbian news texts that focus on ethnification of victims and traffickers. Prior to 2005, the ethnicity of HT victims and perpetrators identified in Serbian HT news was predominantly foreign. The majority of identified HT victims were women from Moldova, Bulgaria, Russia, and Ukraine, whereas the traffickers were especially prominently identified if Albanians (see also Dekić, 2003). This focus on the victims' ethnic origin contributes to exist-ing prejudices, such as the one that trafficked women are naive foreigners from specific countries, and hence responsible for what befell them. This kind of portrayal also promotes victim blaming. As a result, victims of HT are stigmatized, marginalized, denied help and protection, and ultimately deprived of basic human rights.

In this same period (prior to 2005), trafficking as a phenomenon was rarely openly mentioned, obscuring the fact that HT occurs in Serbia and indicating the lack of interest to provide a deep analysis of the issue. Writing about her research into the Serbian news articles (printed from 1998 to 2001) related to women trafficking, Dekić (2003, p. 193) concludes that "an attitude was therefore created in the public mind that trafficking in women happens 'somewhere else'". The same conclusion applies to the impression the media created in the period up to the year 2005. The year 2005 marks a watershed in media representation of HT in Serbia, after which point the majority of identified HT victims were Serbian nationals (in 2006–2007, 73.9% Serbian victims; in 2010, 95% Serbian victims—ASTRA, 2011).

Archetypes and Angles

In structuring a story—news stories included—event participants are con-strued as characters in such a way that both the roles they are given to play and the events themselves "fit in with archetypes of stories" (Bednarek & Caple, 2012, p. 51). In this respect, in HT-related news stories in both languages it is possible to identify the archetypes of heroes, villains, plight, pursuit, rescue, crime, and punishment. Similarly, in media theory, Fulton (2005, pp. 233–234) writes about "'angles' that determine the narrative template" and "seem to be generic, almost universal, ways of ordering our world". In HT news stories in both languages, I identified the following archetypes or angles of representing HT.

[15] For more on characters as stereotypes in news narratives, see Fulton, 2005, p. 238.

A Criminal Act/Act of Organized Crime Story

As the most frequent representation of HT in UK and Serbian print media, this angle treats HT as just another criminal chronicle entry which is interesting while it is current (i.e., "hot") news. News texts in both languages mostly focus on the issues of crime and punishment, presenting very limited information and lacking background information about, for example, details of the illegal operation being run. In the UK press, such examples include articles on a "Sex trafficker facing prison" (*The Sun*, 2015) in which the readers are told only that the trafficker and his gang face jail "for trafficking nearly 100 women to the UK to work in brothels" and the article "Man seized for 'slavery'", stating that "Le, of Deptford, South London, was arrested in Birmingham this week after an inquiry into alleged cannabis production" (*The People*, 2016). It is also added that "Le is also charged with arranging or facilitating the travel of another with a view to exploitation". However, no other information regarding the actual crime of HT is provided. In the Serbian press, criminal acts are reported by representatives of the police force, alleged perpetrators are identified by their first name and first letter of the surname (or initials only), while the victims are unnamed and identified by their age (*Informer*, 2014; *Kurir*, 2013; *Press*, 2012; *Večernje novosti*, 2015a).

In HT news in both languages there is no investigative approach to the issue, nor an analysis of causes, consequences, or the full scale of the problem. It is reasonable to conclude that in some of the texts at least (e.g., in the UK text on illegal immigrants on cannabis farms in the UK), a shift of focus might change public perception, perhaps through including the perspective of HT as a crime against human rights. In Serbian media, some of the questions that should have been more prominently analysed are, for example, the adequacy of punishment for the perpetrators and the suitability of laws under which they are prosecuted. The introduction of anti-HT laws in Serbia, as a non-EU country, has been slow and, as a result, anti-HT efforts are still marred by a very slow or inadequate implementation of the laws in the field.[16] Texts that draw attention to the inadequacy

[16] According to the Human Trafficking Manual for Journalists (issued by ASTRA—a Serbian non-profit anti-HT organization, and OSCE Mission to Serbia), "the state authorities of Serbia and Montenegro placed the problem of HT on the political agenda after the change of political climate in 2000. The US State Department, in its 2001 Trafficking in Persons Report, classified the Republic of Serbia into Tier 3, assessing that it did not fulfil minimum standards in combating HT. One year later, Serbia passed into Tier 2. [...] HT was introduced as a criminal offence into the Criminal Law of Serbia—Article 111b—in April

of laws and, subsequently, punishment, are rare and do not offer any incentive for action, nor do they envisage any solution to the problem. If provided, the answers to these questions might further illustrate the efficacy of the anti-trafficking efforts, pinpoint the weak spots of the legislative foundation, and ultimately lead to its improvement.

A Lucrative Business

Since the explicit mentioning of money is bound to raise interest and provide both shock value and impact value, this is an angle readily taken when representing HT in the British and Serbian press. UK print news state that "[p]eople are making a lot of money. In sexual exploitation, someone can make 1 million pounds a year out of 10 women", or that "One woman could fetch between 6,000 and 8,000 pounds. She could then earn her buyer 800 pounds a day" (Taylor, 2007; *The Daily Telegraph*, 2015). In Serbian media, such information is placed in the headlines: "People traffickers in Serbia earning millions of euros from prostitution", "People traffickers earn slightly less than drug lords", "Jočić: HT fetches as much as 13 billion dollars a year", "60 billion euro per year in HT" (*Blic*, 2011; *Dnevnik*, 2007; *Glas javnosti*, 2007; *Press*, 2009). Again, what is evident is the problem of perspective—the focus is not on the victims, but on the business aspect of the crime. Additionally, in Serbian media, HT is presented as a lucrative business with minimal risks due to the abovementioned gaps in the legal system.

Sensational News

The third angle taken with HT representation is that of the sensationalist coverage of the issue. This is especially evident in Serbian media, in which all the gory and scandalous details of women trafficking are emphasized, as in the aforementioned cases of underage victims, victims trafficked by the members of their family, or victims sold into prostitution for ridiculous amounts of money and/or other material possessions. These articles also focus on methods of coercion, underlining the brutality of these crimes but also convincing the public that the women in question are indeed

2003. [...] On 1 January 2006, the new Criminal Code of Serbia came into force. In Article 388, it introduced some novelties into the definition of human trafficking and new penal provisions for this offence, distinguishing it clearly from people smuggling". For more on the legislative and institutional framework for tackling HT in Serbia in, see the *Human Trafficking Manual for Journalists* (2008).

victims, as if otherwise they would not be believed, for various cultural reasons. This is indicative of victims' perceived position, credibility, and ultimately their basic human rights. Similarly, the UK press featured an article on a human traffickers' camp ("the makeshift jail, made of bamboo and barbed wire" "that may have held up to 300 people") discovered in the Malaysian jungle (Freeman, 2015). The camp was equipped with cages that held prisoners, and the camping ground was scattered with human remains, "including a jaw bone". Although the torturing methods of these human traffickers are repulsive and certainly draw attention to the mechanisms used by the trafficking syndicates to force their victims into submission, there is also no doubt that the newspaper article focuses on the sensationalist approach in its choice of perspective and journalistic angle. Foregrounding shocking aspects is a simplistic approach that pushes the real causes of HT to the background.

Text and Narration

Text Structure

As Bednarek and Caple (2012, p. 96) posit, a typical news text consists of three parts: headline, intro/lead, and body/lead development. The headline and intro/lead serve to "frame the event, summarize the story and attract readers", also construing newsworthiness (Bednarek & Caple, 2012, pp. 96–97).[17] A good example of how the choice of headlines draws attention to particular aspects of the event and implies ideological positioning is found in the Serbian corpus. On 26 March 2013, three newspapers published stories regarding the same event, a 16-year-old girl being forced into prostitution by the gang of four for one month (*Blic*, 2013a; *Informer*, 2013; *Kurir*, 2013). All three headlines emphasize the force used against the victim. Other than that, the journalists chose to emphasize different aspects of this crime. In the articles headlined "They forced a little girl into prostitution!" and "A child forced into prostitution!", both the act of forced prostitution and the age of the victim are highlighted, emphasising the story's shock value. The sensationalist aspect in both articles is further enhanced by the exclamation mark. One headline, however, opts for disclosing the sex of the victim ("little girl"), while the

---

[17] Bednarek and Caple (2012, p. 97) here also acknowledge the fact that the headline and intro/lead are frequently seen as "one unit" called "abstract" or "nucleus".

other focuses on the fact that the victim was a child, not stating the sex, thus removing any association with sexual activities (as completely inconceivable for children in general) and implying the damage done to the childhood innocence. The headline "A teenager force-solicited for a month" presents the victim as significantly older ("a teenager") and thus the possibility of sexual activities is not automatically excluded for the victim, which might make the criminal act slightly less grave (or at least slightly less shocking) in the eyes of the readership. The focus is, however, placed on the length of the molestation period ("a month"). While the previous two headlines are given in the passive voice, placing focus on the victim and not the perpetrators, in the third headline the guilt of perpetrators (and not the suffering of the victim) is stressed.

In standard journalism, events are not presented chronologically. Instead, information about these events is ordered according to its significance, following the inverted pyramid structure (Bednarek & Caple, 2012, p. 100; Fulton, 2005, p. 228): the news lead provides a summary of the event, followed by crucial details and quotations, whereas the least important details are placed at the end of the text. In this respect, Meilby (1996, p. 254) distinguishes between four main groups of information according to their dissemination: introduction (new, important information), background (provides perspective for the information), documentation (usually quotes), and filling (information that could be left out). News stories on HT in both languages generally follow this organizing principle, with one crucial exception—contextual information, necessary to evaluate the news, is placed at the very end of the story. One such example is found the UK text headlined "Children forced into Oliver Twist thieving" (*The Daily Telegraph*, 2015), with the following closing remark: "The Home Office estimated in December that there were up to 13,000 victims in the UK, and Mr Hyland said there were 151 convictions last year". This final sentence, instead of containing "filler" information, provides additional context for interpretation (through contrasting the number of victims to the number of convictions), and proves necessary for the intended meaning (implicitly showing the lack of success when responding to HT). In the Serbian article on "Men increasingly becoming victims of HT" (*Politika*, 2009b), the text presents a study done by the Victimological Society of Serbia and provides information on the number of male victims identified in one year (407 victims in 2003). The closing remark emphasizes the lack of a state registry of the male trafficking cases and of a support network for the victims, while drawing attention to the misconstrued public image of a typical trafficking victim as being female. The closing part of the text, thus, provides a crucial insight into the problem and encourages the wider definition of both HT and its victim profile.

Levels of Narration

Both UK and Serbian articles on HT typically feature two levels of narration: the frame/primary text (commonly a testimony, commentary, or report made by a primary source of information) and the embedded text (featuring the act of trafficking and/or criminal acts committed by the trafficked people).[18] A UK press example headlined "Girl 'passed round 60 men in sex ring'" (Elsk, 2015) brings the report on a court hearing of "eleven men on trial" accused of "multiple rape of a child under 13, child prostitution" and other offences related to the crime. While the primary text features a statement by "Oliver Saxby, QC, for the prosecution" (as an official source) on the trial itself, the embedded text brings details of the crime (the abuse of the child and her friend by 60 men in sex abuse gang, the targeting, grooming, drugging and molestation details). Such division on the level of narration mirrors the choice of focalization on the level of the story, since the focalizers are "placed" within the primary text, while the characters are positioned within the embedded text. In the Serbian article about the sex trafficking of a teenage girl (*Blic*, 2013a), the frame text features the police arrest of four people suspected of this crime and a one-month custody they received at the initial court hearing. The embedded text brings the story of the crime—the beatings, threats and soliciting the victim had to endure. What this suggests about the text's ideological viewpoint is that the focus is on the consequences of the crime and on those who have the power to deal with those consequences (the police force, judicial system, government institutions), not on the roots of the crime and the analysis of those circumstances that led to victims being vulnerable in the first place.

---

[18] Bal (2009, p. 73) refers to the primary text as "the narrator's text" and to the embedded text as "the actor's text", stating that their hierarchical position is indicated "by the fundamental principle of level".

Genre

McNair (1998, pp. 9–10) distinguishes between five basic forms of journalistic output: news report/fact report, feature article (equivalent to the
documentary; in-depth reportage/analysis), commentary/column
(authoritative viewpoint on an issue), interview, and editorial (a newspa-
per/periodical that "speaks out" in its "public voice"). The most frequent, and indeed dominant, journalistic genre in articles on HT in both
languages is that of news report, which reduces the issue of HT to several
lines of fact-oriented announcements that do not portray HT in any
depth. The least frequently seen are pieces of investigative journalism that
would investigate factors leading to and governing the process of
HT. Some of these factors might include economic, political, and social
issues, such as: loss of jobs, poverty, existential crises, lack of laws, poor
implementation of the laws, violence against women, lack of human
rights, and general criminal activities and tendencies. On the other hand,
HT might be linked to region-specific events: wars, general instability,
foreign activities and influences, and forced or voluntary migration.
Investigation into these roots, however, is missing from the texts on HT
in both languages. This conclusion is in accordance with the general tendency in standard journalism, which states that economic factors and market forces direct the present-day journalism towards pure fact reports and
away from investigative journalism as a not so cost-efficient genre (cf.
Fulton, 2005, pp. 224–225).

IDEOLOGICAL POSITIONING

As Soderlund (2002, p. 441) indicates, news reports present "a site of
cultural production that operates according to institutional and professional rules and paradigms and within dominant political ideologies".
While the previous aspects of analysis show the workings of these rules and
paradigms of the journalistic profession when creating news texts on HT,
and thus answer the question of how the intended meaning is created and
how, subsequently, the ideological position underlying such creation is
indicated, this section shows what this ideological position is and why it is
present in the first place.

McNair (1998, p. 5) maintains that there is no such thing as creating
news without making deliberate choices when selecting and contextual-
izing facts. Hence, reality is never simply reflected in the news accounts,

nor are journalists simply independent and objective recorders of events (Bird & Dardenne 1988, p. 66; Johnson-Cartee, 2005, p. 157). Since placing emphasis and creating focus implies a certain standpoint, the process of news construction necessarily creates bias and promotes an agenda. In questioning the agenda when creating a story we, as readers, are conducting what Walter Fisher (1970, p. 131) refers to as a "motive analysis". According to him, an author always has a reason, or reasons, for putting a narrative before an audience. These reasons, or motives, not only determine the content of the narrative, but also the manner of its construction and delivery. The content is never devoid of "an attitude about that content" (Fisher, 1970, p. 132). Thus, every narrative "expresses a theme or thesis, an inference of judgment, which is to be preferred above any other proposition or proposal that relates to its subject matter" (Fisher, 1970, p. 131). In passing this judgement, "journalism, therefore, like any other narrative which is the work of human agency" becomes "essentially *ideological*—a communicative vehicle for the transmission to an audience not just of facts but of the assumptions, beliefs and values of its maker(s), drawn from and expressive of a particular world-view" (McNair, 1998, p. 6).

In news media texts in both languages, the framing of HT—as a social, political, and public issue—prompts a particular response both on the part of the public and that of governmental institutions. Framing of HT as a criminal activity draws attention away from the economic, political, and social roots of the problem and reduces a very complex issue to a simple one that can be tackled through the application of a range of policing and law enforcement measures. Writing about UN anti-trafficking policy in Bosnia and Herzegovina, Vandenberg (2007, p. 92) questions the effect this type of media coverage has on HT, envisaging increased policing as the response to the rise in media coverage of trafficking activities. According to her, aggressive policing might produce greater negative consequences for the trafficked individuals than for the traffickers.

Ethnification of characters in reports on HT in both languages creates a misguided impression that HT is an imported problem, legitimizes calls for strict immigration laws, and creates tension between the domestic population and immigrants. Media prioritization of sex trafficking and women trafficking over other types of trafficking promotes the gender aspect of the problem and contributes to the further victimization of women and forced sex workers, establishing a cause and effect link between prostitution and trafficking (Chang & Kim, 2007, p. 3). Additionally, it creates the need for strict anti-prostitution laws, which again diverts attention from investigation into the broader phenomenon of trafficking and identification of "factors that facilitate trafficking, such as poverty, discrimination, and civil and political unrest" (Chang & Kim, 2007, p. 3) of certain regions. Unlike the UK, which serves as a destination country, Serbia's role in human trafficking is currently three-fold: it serves as a country of origin (mostly for women trafficked into Bosnia, Kosovo, Macedonia, West Europe), a destination country, and a key transit country in the Balkans (for victims trafficked into Italy, Spain, and France via Bosnia, or to the Near East via Kosovo and Macedonia). Although Serbian news media emphasize the need to investigate the factors that make victims, especially women, vulnerable to traffickers, this investigation is missing from the news texts. The issues such as poor economic situation (in the post-Soviet and post-Eastern bloc countries), high tolerance of violence against women, militarization of the regions, and great social and political disturbance of the 1990s and 2000s, appear to be problems better left untouched.

All the measures and actions devised or called for by the framing of HT focus on its effects, not causes. In this way, in Kempadoo's words (2005, p. xiv), "neoliberal economic interests of corporations, multilateral agencies, policy experts and national governments" remain protected, "rather than those of the world's working and poor people".

CONCLUSION

The treatment of narrative elements and narrative structure determines the focus of the news media texts. Most articles on HT, in both languages, place the primary focus on arrests, court proceedings, and government announcements, with a secondary focus on the act of trafficking itself. The media's reliance on official sources leads to bureaucratization of the news on HT and necessarily implies the ideological position taken by news agencies. Alternative points of view, such as those belonging to the academics or activists in the field, are either completely excluded or awarded a far less prominent position. This minimizes the role and the influence other sectors might have in producing legislative acts and public policies relevant for dealing with HT and steers the public towards establishment-provided viewpoints. Additionally, the media framing of HT and insistence on the few chosen paradigms seriously obstructs the public perception of the problem and limits both the interest and the influence that more extensive public debate might provide. The public agenda on HT shaped in this way by the print news media, both in UK and Serbia, suggests strong inclination towards retaining the status quo of political power relations and economic interests.

REFERENCES

ASTRA. (2008). *Human trafficking manual for journalists.* Belgrade: ASTRA.
ASTRA. (2011). *Human trafficking in the Republic of Serbia: Report for the period 2000–2010.* Belgrade: ASTRA.
Badcock, J. (2015, May 9). Excess baggage: Boy smuggled in a suitcase. *The Daily Telegraph*, [no pagination].
Bal, M. (2009). *Narratology: Introduction to the theory of narrative.* (3rd ed.). Toronto: University of Toronto Press.
Bednarek, M., & Caple, H. (2012). *News discourse.* London: Continuum.
Bednarek, M., & Caple, H. (2017). *The discourse of news values: How news organizations create newsworthiness.* New York: Oxford University Press.
Bird, S. E., & Dardenne, R. W. (1988). Myth, chronicle and story: Exploring the narrative qualities of news. In J. W. Carey (ed.), *Media, myth, and narratives: Television and the press* (pp. 67–86). London: Sage.
Blic. (2004, August 8). Trgovina ljudima u Srbiji, [no pagination].
Blic. (2011, July 24). Trgovci ljudima po zaradi posle rasturača narkotika, [no pagination].
Blic. (2013a, March 26). Tinejdžerku mesec dana silom podvodili, [no pagination].
Blic. (2013b, September 17). Prodao mladu za 1.000 evra, [no pagination].
Butler, P., & Bowcott, O. (2013, November 22). Call for help was first step to freedom. *The Guardian*, p. 3.
Chang, G., & Kim, K. (2007). Reconceptualizing approaches to human trafficking: New directions and perspectives from the field(s). *Stanford Journal of Civil Rights and Civil Liberties, 3*, 317.
Clark, A. (2001, April 21). Slavery summit: Confectioners pledge to halt cocoa farm abuse. *The Guardian*, [no pagination].
Conboy, M. (2007). *The language of the news.* New York: Routledge.
Danas. (2003, September 23). Oko 200.000 žena u švercerskoj mreži, [no pagination].
Danas. (2004a, January 29). Godišnje od 700 hiljada do dva miliona žrtava, [no pagination].
Danas. (2004b, May 8). Tri godine zatvora za šverc ljudi, [no pagination].
Danas. (2004c, December 1). Uvredljiv tretman žrtve, [no pagination].
Danas. (2005, November 4). Godišnje se preprodaje dva do četiri miliona ljudi, [no pagination].

Danas. (2015, March 4). Osuđeni za trgovinu ljudima, [no pagination].

Dekić, S. (2003). Sex, slavery and politics: Representations of trafficked women in the Serbian media. *Journal of Canadian Women's Studies, 22*(3/4), 192–200.

Dnevnik. (2007, October 19). Jočić: Od trgovine ljudima godišnje i do 13 milijardi dolara, [no pagination].

Dnevnik. (2009, October 19). Kad "momci" nestaju, robovlasnici propadaju, [no pagination].

Dnevnik. (2014, August 1). Proleteri ugroženiji nego seksualne radnice, [no pagination].

Elsk, S. (2015, May 19). Girl 'passed round 60 men in sex ring'. *The Times*, p. 20.

Fearn, H. (2015, May 16). 'Trafficked' Briton to lodge drugs death-sentence appeal. *The Independent*, p. 16.

Fisher, W. R. (1970). A motive view of communication. *Quarterly Journal of Speech, 56*, 131–139.

Freeman, C. (2015, May 27). Cages found at jungle traffickers' camp. *The Daily Telegraph*, p. 16.

Fulton, H. (2005). Introduction: The power of narrative. In H. Fulton, R. Huisman, J. Murphet, & A. Dunn (eds.), *Narrative and media* (pp. 1–8). Cambridge: Cambridge University Press.

Galtung, J., & Ruge, M. (1981). Structuring and selecting news. In S. Cohen & J. Young (eds.), *The manufacture of news* (pp. 57–72). London: Constable.

Glas javnosti. (2004a, August 4). Kako se zaštititi od trgovaca ljudima, [no pagination].

Glas javnosti. (2004b, November 2). U svetu godišnje oko 700.000 prodatih ljudi, [no pagination].

Glas javnosti. (2007, November 11). Obrne se i 60 milijardi evra godišnje, [no pagination].

Harrison, D. (2007, March 18). Reid out to crush 21st-century slave trade. *The Daily Telegraph*, [no pagination].

Informer. (2013, March 26). Terali devojčicu na prostituciju! [no pagination].

Informer. (2014, March 15). Vlasnik luna-parka 4 godine imao roba, [no pagination].

Jahn, M. (2005). *Narratology: A guide to the theory of narrative.* Cologne: University of Cologne.

Johnson-Cartee, K. S. (2005). *News narratives and news framing: Constructing political reality.* Lanham: Rowman & Littlefield.

Kelly, A., & Scruton, P. (2015, April 2). Domestic workers: 47 million people worldwide denied basic labour rights. *The Guardian*, [no pagination].

Kempadoo, K. (2005). Introduction: From moral panic to global justice: Changing perspectives on trafficking. In K. Kempadoo (ed.), *Trafficking and prostitution reconsidered: New perspectives on migration, sex work, and human rights* (pp. vii–xxxiv). Boulder: Paradigm Publishers.

Kurir. (2012, June 26). Vorlik: iskorenite savremeno ropstvo, [no pagination].

Kurir. (2013, March 26). Dete terali na prostituciju! [no pagination].

Kweifio-Okai, C. (2015, June 12). Five myths about child labour. *The Guardian,* [no pagination].

Leonard, T. (2001, April 6). 14 years for trucker who left 58 to die. *The Daily Star,* p. 8.

Marsden, S. (2015, April 7). I was trafficked by Westminster sex abuse ring. *The Daily Mail,* p. 10.

McNair, B. (1998). *The sociology of journalism.* London: Arnold.

Meilby, M. (1996). *Journalistikkens grundtrin.* Arhus: Forlaget Ajour. Quoted in: E. Grunwald (2005). "Narrative Norms in Written News". *Nordicom Review,* 26(1), 63–79.

Naše novine. (2014, August 5). Najveće žrtve trgovine ljudima su—građevinci! [no pagination].

Nedeljni telegraf. (2008, September 24). Srbija u odlučnoj borbi protiv trgovine ljudima, [no pagination].

Phillips, M. (2013, November 2). Persecution and poverty driving gypsies of Romania to Britain. *The Sun,* pp. 44–45.

Politika. (2004, June 4). Stop trgovini i krijumčarenju ljudi, [no pagination].

Politika. (2006, December 8). Strategija borbe protiv trgovine ljudima, [no pagination].

Politika. (2007, August 21). Moldavija, zemlja seksualnog ropstva, [no pagination].

Politika. (2009a, January 5). Žrtva je i muškog roda, [no pagination].

Politika. (2009b, September 24). Muškarci sve više žrtve trgovine ljudima, [no pagination].

Politika. (2009c, October 19). Dan borbe protiv trgovine ljudima, [no pagination].

Politika. (2009d, October 29). Hajka na otmičare, [no pagination].

Pravda. (2010, October 18). Filmom protiv organizovanog kriminala, [no pagination].

Pregled. (2011, July 18). Domaći državljani na meti, [no pagination].

Press. (2009, July 27). Tužilac: Trgovci ljudima u Srbiji zarađuju milione evra na prostituciji, [no pagination].

Press. (2012, September 26). Prodao trudnu ženu za 1.500 evra, pa prijavio da je oteta, [no pagination].

Rankin, J. (2016, May 19). Human traffickers 'using migration crisis' to force more people into slavery. *The Guardian,* [no pagination].

Smith, H. (2015, August 20). UK police deployed to Calais to tackle people-trafficking gangs, p. 19.

Soderlund, G. (2002). Covering urban vice: The New York Times, "White slavery," and the construction of journalistic knowledge. *Critical Studies in Media Communication, 19,* 438–460.

Squires, N. (2016, May 30). Hundreds of migrants drown in deadliest week in Mediterranean this year. *The Daily Telegraph*, p. 16.

Stockwell, S. (1999). Beyond the fourth estate: Democracy, deliberation and journalism theory. *Australian Journalism Review, 21*(1), 38.

Tannen, D. (1993). *Framing in discourse.* Oxford: Oxford University Press.

Taylor, B. (2007, March 8). Women for sale in the Gatwick slave auctions. *The Daily Mail*, p. 41.

The Daily Mail. (2015, April 8). Baby is 'sold' for £6,500 and a BMW, p. 26.

The Daily Mail. (2016, May 30). Pope slams 'blood sucker' bosses, p. 33.

The Daily Star. (2008, March 8). Halt this Evil Trade, p. 6.

The Daily Star. (2016, May 23). 28 illegals in a lorry, p. 2.

The Daily Telegraph. (2013, November 13). 348 held over Canadian child porn, p. 22.

The Daily Telegraph. (2015, June 1). Children forced into Oliver Twist thieving, warns anti-slavery chief, p. 11.

The Guardian. (2015, June 27). Man charged with human trafficking after raid rescues Romanian woman, [no pagination].

The People. (2016, May 29). Man seized for 'slavery', p. 9.

The Sun. (2015, July 17). Sex trafficker facing prison, p. 14.

The Times. (2007, March 24). Police fear Olympics will lure sex slave traffickers, p. 15.

Usborne, D. (2005, May 12). Scandal of the 'slaves' who pamper the nails of rich New Yorkers. *The Independent*, p. 24.

Vandenberg, M. E. (2007). Peacekeeping and rule breaking: United Nations anti-trafficking policy in Bosnia and Herzegovina. In H. Richard Friman & S. Reich (eds.), *Human trafficking, human security, and the Balkans* (pp. 81–95). Pittsburgh: University of Pittsburgh Press.

Večernje novosti. (2004a, October 20). Svedočenje bez okrivljenih, [no pagination].

Večernje novosti. (2004b, December 1). Vređaju Moldavku, [no pagination].

Večernje novosti. (2007a, November 10). I muškarci roblje, [no pagination].

Večernje novosti. (2007b, November 25). Bilo jednom na Balkanu, [no pagination].

Večernje novosti. (2015a, April 16). Prodao devojku za laptop i 100€, [no pagination].

Večernje novosti. (2015b, June 2). Uhapšeno 13 osoba, [no pagination].

Watt, N., Travis, A., & Mason, R. (2015, June 17). Britain to send intelligence officers to Sicily to 'disrupt' human traffickers, [no pagination].

Zelizer, B., & Allan, S. (2010). *Keywords in news and journalism studies.* Maidenhead: Open University Press.

CHAPTER 4

"In the Suitcase was a Boy": Representing Transnational Child Trafficking in Contemporary Crime Fiction

Charlotte Beyer

Abstract This chapter investigates representations of transnational child trafficking in contemporary crime fiction, focusing specifically on the depiction of child trafficking and its victims. Beyer examines the role of crime fiction in raising reader awareness of human trafficking and of the child victims' predicament and plight, considering didactic dimensions of the genre and how it tends to erase victims in the aftermath of crime. Through detailed examinations of representations of child trafficking and its social and cultural contexts in selected post-2000 British and Scandinavian crime fiction texts, the chapter argues that crime fiction can be seen to engage explicitly in public and private debates around human trafficking, and, through its popular outreach, has the potential to affect popular perceptions of human trafficking and its victims.

Keywords Crime fiction • Educational • Gender • Narrative • Plot • Transnational child trafficking • Trauma • Violence

C. Beyer (✉)
University of Gloucestershire, Cheltenham, UK
e-mail: cbeyer@glos.ac.uk

© The Author(s) 2018
C. Gregoriou (ed.), *Representations of Transnational Human Trafficking*, https://doi.org/10.1007/978-3-319-78214-0_4

Introduction: Exploring Representations of Child Trafficking

Since the agreement of the Palermo Protocol in 2000, there has been an increased interest in the topic of transnational human trafficking, particularly in in the news media, but also in documentary programmes and crime fiction (Gregoriou & Ras, 2018; Dearey, 2018).[1] This growing awareness of human trafficking has recently resulted in academic research into its representation. Notably, in 2016, the *Anti-Trafficking Review* journal devoted a special issue to the topic of "trafficking representations". However, while offering a number of articles examining the subject of the representation of human trafficking, the *Anti-Trafficking Review* issue included no examinations of crime fiction, or literary fiction. Similarly, scholarly investigations of transnational child trafficking representations are lacking, or considered together with adult female sex trafficking (Moore & Goldberg, 2015). The neglect by critics of representations of child trafficking in contemporary crime fiction is puzzling because the genre offers thought-provoking and challenging depictions of different forms of child trafficking in a popular and generally accessible medium.

This chapter aims to redress this absence by offering a critical examination of representations of transnational child trafficking (TCT) in post-2000 British and Scandinavian crime fiction novels. The representation of TCT in crime fiction (and literary fiction) has rarely received any sustained critical attention (with the notable exceptions of Moore and Goldberg (2015) and Bickford (2010, 2012). Importantly, therefore, this chapter offers a critical assessment of these representations and their wider cultural significance, by examining child trafficking narratives in selected crime fiction novels. Crime fiction enjoys a wide readership, and the representations generated by these books can potentially have a significant impact on public awareness of TCT. It is, therefore, pertinent to investigate portrayals of TCT in crime fiction, in order to analyse and understand these fictional representations and their effect, and to understand the social, cultural, and literary contexts for those representations. Through a critical analysis of depictions of TCT in crime fiction, this chapter identifies clichéd narrative patterns that frequently occur in crime fiction treating the subject of child trafficking, as well as tracing those representations that offer more complex and nuanced portrayals of TCT victims, their agency, resilience, and survival.

[1] The title quotation is from Kaaberbøl and Friis (2008, 2011, p. 2).

METHODOLOGY AND CONTEXT

In this chapter I investigate representations of TCT in a selection of British and Scandinavian crime fiction novels: Marnie Riches' *The Girl who Walked in the Shadows* (2016), Ruth Dugdall's *Nowhere Girl* (2015), Lene Kaaberbøl and Agnete Friis' *The Boy in the Suitcase* (2008, 2011), Emelie Schepp's (2014, 2016) novel *Marked for Life*, and Minette Walters' *The Cellar* (2015). Additional references are made to other selected crime novels offering relevant representations of TCT, where appropriate to the discussion and to offer context. The above listed novels were selected for analysis due to the complex and nuanced representations of TCT they offer. TCT is a global phenomenon, and a number of novels from America and the Global South treat this subject, as well as the Western European texts selected for analysis here (Bickford, 2010; Moore & Goldberg, 2015). For the purposes of this present investigation, concentrating on TCT as a theme in European crime fiction enables us to examine the (self-perceived) role of Europe as the destination (Jacomella, 2010, p. 4) for migrants, refugees, and trafficking victims, typically from the Global South but also from former Eastern Bloc countries, and to assess how literature and popular culture convey the important questions relating to human security and rights currently posed by human trafficking (Jonsson, 2009, p. 7).

In post-2000 crime fiction, representations of transnational sex trafficking (rather than forced labour), reflect prevailing media attitudes (Gregoriou & Ras, 2018; Muždeka, 2018; Moore & Goldberg, 2015). These stereotypes of sex trafficking of women can be observed in crime novels such as Stuart Neville, *Stolen Souls* (2011) and Stieg Larsson's *The Girl Who Played with Fire* (2006, 2009) among others, reflecting Ruivo's assertion that, "human trafficking continues to be largely associated with sexual exploitation" (2015, p. 22). However, the distinction between adult sex trafficking and child sex trafficking is at times erased, both in fiction and by critics referring to trafficked "women and girls" (Moore & Goldberg, 2015). Matt Johnson's *Deadly Game* (2017) exemplifies a portrayal of female sex trafficking where the key female victim is a TCT victim, although this is not acknowledged in the novel. *Deadly Game* states on the opening page that the female victim was 17 when she was trafficked, thus underage according to the Palermo Protocol which states 18 as the age of consent and adulthood.[2]

---

[2] The Palermo Protocol defines child trafficking as the "recruitment, transportation, transfer, harbouring or receipt" of a child under the age of 18 for the purpose of exploitation; see Protocol (2000).

This conflation of women and underage girls is problematic in considering representations of TCT, as it erases an important boundary regarding consent. The popular fixation with sex trafficking themes can also be seen in several other post-2000 crime fictions dealing with TCT plots, such as Liz Mistry's *Unquiet Souls* (2016) and Marnie Riches' *The Girl who Walked in the Shadows*. However, as the crime novels discussed in this chapter demonstrate, children are trafficked for a variety of purposes, as Fussey and Rawlinson also note: "Children are trafficked for diverse purposes, not only for commercial sexual exploitation, such as prostitution and pornography, but also servitude, forced labour, criminality, peonage and illicit military recruitment" (2017, p. 16; Bulman, 2017a). While acknowledging child sex trafficking representations, my chapter seeks to expand the investigation of TCT motifs, to include a range of other purposes, such as organ trafficking, child soldiering, modern slavery, and domestic slavery. This investigation of broader TCT themes assesses the impact of crime fiction authors depicting a range of non-sexual trafficking crimes, thus challenging a monolithic focus on sex trafficking.

TCT, the subject of my present investigation, requires particular attention, since as Pearce, Hynes, and Bovarnick state "the trafficking of children and young people […] constitutes one of the most serious human rights violations of our time" (2013, p. 2). The seriousness of human trafficking is underlined by Ruivo, who describes it as an opportunistic crime exploiting the weak and powerless: "Traffickers and recruiters take advantage of the social and economic fragilities of countries, seeking their victims among those with financial difficulties in countries with high rates of unemployment and poverty, as well as lower levels of education" (2015, pp. 21–22). Yet the individuality and humanity of victims often appear to be erased through stereotypical representations of human trafficking (Gregoriou & Ras, 2018). However, the importance of rendering trafficking victims visible is reflected in a 2017 feature in *The Guardian*. Under the title, "Traffickers take all that makes you human: faces of modern slavery", Kelly and Hodal's article (2017) uses photos of victims and their personal stories and experiences of human trafficking to make its point. The insistence on the humanity of trafficking victims is vital because it counters the move towards erasure and anonymisation of victims and their dignity otherwise seen in news media reportage on the subject (Gregoriou & Ras, 2018). This chapter extends this preoccupation with the visibility of trafficking victims, specifically children, by using crime fiction novels to examine the politics of their representation.

Employing a range of critical perspectives to examine themes in crime fiction of TCT, trauma, and victimhood specifically in relation to children, my chapter contributes to an emerging critical field.[3] In investigating the selected crime novels and assessing the politics of representation, this chapter's methodology is focused around three areas: identification of types of TCT; crime fiction as a site for the representation of trauma and victimhood; and uses of crime fiction subgenres and/or narrative patterns. The purpose of this multi-faceted approach is to heighten understanding of the power of linguistic and fictional representation in creating complex representations of TCT, and to examine the role and function of crime fiction in shaping and influencing readers' understanding of TCT. The chapter draws on Fussey and Rawlinson's (2017) discussion of narrative patterns utilised to depict victimhood and agency in popular discourses around child trafficking. My analysis focuses specifically on thematic and discursive constructions of TCT victims, considering how conventional narrative patterns of heroism, abduction, and rescue are reflected, reproduced, or resisted in crime fiction novels, and to what effect. Fussey and Rawlinson refer to Propp's analysis of patterns of heroic rescue in folktales to illustrate how such motifs dominate representations of child victims in trafficking narratives (2017, p. 55).[4] The critique of stereotypical representations of trafficking victims and perpetrators by Kinney (2014), in her discussion of popular cultural texts and their depiction of human trafficking, has proved useful for analysing cultural responses to trafficking crimes. Other analyses of fictional portrayals of human trafficking include Moore and Goldberg (2015) and Bickford (2012). Cree, Clapton, and Smith examine representation of TCT and sexual exploitation in the twenty-first century, looking at the different kinds of exploitation children are subjected to and their countries of origin, concluding that stereotypical representations of TCT tend to depict the children as without agency (2014, p. 431). Such narrative patterns and positions are examined in the crime fictions analysed here, in order to assess whether portrayals of TCT offer stereotypical or alternative narratives and positions for victims, and how these representations may contribute to readers' and the wider public's knowledge of TCT.

---

[3] See also Bickford (2012) for an examination of the relationship between narrative and public perception of trafficking.

[4] Fussey and Rawlinson refer to Propp's *Morphology of the Folktale* (1968) [1928].

My narrative analysis of the selected crime novels focuses specifically on the representation of child victims of trafficking, their experiences of trauma, and the literary language and techniques used to portray these experiences. This chapter draws on Bloom for an understanding of what constitutes trauma in children and how trauma manifests itself, and on Dodd and Vickroy for analyses of strategies used in literature to depict trauma. My investigation extends Dodd's argument that "[c]rime fiction opens up a space in which to depict more authentic and safe representations of traumatic experience to a willing and receptive audience" (2015, p. 5). The discussion of trauma and victimhood reflects Fussey and Rawlinson's insight that views of TCT are defined or shaped by "Western notions of innocence, guilt, childhood, and of the status of 'deserving' victim" (2017, p. 16). The narrative patterns, character portrayals, and detailed depictions of trauma in the selected novels are vital to their representation of TCT. I argue that these portrayals are integral to the genre's capacity to address the complexity of TCT to different audiences and readerships who are not necessarily knowledgeable about human trafficking, and to engender a sense of reader empathy for child victims of trafficking. As Bickford argues, "These novels can generate empathy and outrage, and they provide perspectives, information and analyses that can lead to a commitment to make change" (2012, p. 134). I argue that the depiction of child trauma plays a central role in conveying to the reader the suffering caused by TCT, and confronting them with the high individual and collective cost of this crime.

I draw on crime fiction criticism to underpin my identification of subgenres used in the crime novels under analysis. To that end, the crime fiction criticism by Worthington (2011) and Brunsdale (2016) provides genre-specific critiques of narrative elements and the use of subgenres in crime fiction. Crime fiction subgenres play an important part in drawing the reader's focus to a particular dimension of the novel, such as narrative perspective, psychological aspects, or the setting, thus framing and shaping TCT representations. This analysis considers the social critique articulated in these crime fictions, and the impact of the representations they offer on the reader's and general public's understanding of human trafficking, its causes, and its effects on victims. Brunsdale's (2016) examination of trafficking themes in Scandinavian crime fiction provides context for the Nordic Noir novels examined here. Worthington's (2011) and Bickford's (2010, 2012) analyses are useful in assessing the didactic dimensions of crime fiction, and reflecting on its capacity to affect readers' awareness of and engagement with significant public issues such as human trafficking. Crime fiction combines a narrative centred around generating suspense and mental problem-solving with realistic and affecting portrayals of crime and how crime impacts the individual and society, educating readers and the wider public about human trafficking. However, crime fiction novels may also struggle to reconcile a suspense-driven plot focused on entertainment with a realistic portrayal of TCT and its victims through the depiction of their trauma, and this is a question my chapter engages with. Through this multi-faceted critical approach blending crime fiction criticism with sociological and cultural analyses of human trafficking and theories about trauma and its representation, my analysis engenders a specific focus on the politics of representation and the capacity of crime fiction to create greater awareness of human trafficking, particularly TCT.

Child Sex Trafficking

Riches' *The Girl who Walked in the Shadows* (2016)[5] primarily portrays transnational child sex trafficking and child abduction, but also alludes to historical child sex trafficking crimes. Set in Britain, Germany, and Holland, *Girl* uses its British and European settings to represent complex contemporary Western European societies characterised by inequality, social tension, violence and brutality, and opportunistic crime. The novel's black female investigator character, Dr George McKenzie, is also an academic.[6] George is a research fellow in Criminology at Cambridge University but also carries out work for the Home Office (Riches, 2016, Part 1, Chap. 4), and is asked to assist the Dutch police with profiling a murderer. This leads to George's involvement in the investigation of the disappearance of two young children, kidnapped from their parents' back garden. Their search uncovers a TCT ring where which acquires young children from Roma camps, who they then sell for sexual abuse, slave labour, and organ trafficking (Riches, 2016, Part 3, Chap. 45). *Girl*'s trafficking plot is split into two separate storylines, a duality that reflects apparent contradictions in fictional representations of child trafficking based around perceptions of class and ethnicity. One plotline concerns the kidnapping of children from a socially privileged family. The other plotline concerns the organised

---

[5] From here on referred to as *Girl*.
[6] Riches' use of a BAME protagonist connects with her own background which she describes as "minority ethnic" (Diamond, 2016).

transnational trafficking of a large number of children from Eastern Europe, primarily for sexual exploitation. *Girl* also depicts historic domestic child sex trafficking of children in the 1960s, 1970s and 1980s in Northern England, through George's research into the subject (Riches, 2016, Part 1, Chap. 2).[7] These descriptions of historic and contemporary child sex trafficking in Europe, both transnational and domestic, reflect current media debates and their focus on sexual exploitation.[8]

The TCT plotline in *Girl* focuses primarily on the trafficking and exploitation of Roma children. The novel incorporates a discussion between George and another researcher, Sophie, about the trafficking of Roma children, explaining that the stereotypes and media representations surrounding the Roma, which hold them responsible for child abductions and trafficking, are far removed from the reality, which is that Roma children from south Eastern Europe are the most frequent victims of trafficking (Riches, 2016, Part 1, Chap. 9). Sophie explains to George that:

> the kids trafficked out of Bulgaria, the Czech Republic, Hungary, Romania and Slovakia, Roma kids constitute about seventy per cent. They're disproportionately poor. Maybe someone trusted in the family or village offers to get a child work elsewhere. [...] movement of children over borders into brothels, sweatshops, begging on the streets. (Riches, 2016, Part 1, Chap. 9)

Explaining the context to *Girl*'s portrayal of this subject, Fussey and Rawlinson state,

> The Romani people [...] face a compounded victimisation: as collective 'collateral damage' of the economic and social insecurity that has accompanied neoliberal policies especially as exacerbated by the global economic crisis, and additionally as direct victims of the growing levels of poverty that have resulted from the crisis. (2017, p. 12)

Girl's representation of current debates around TCT, and its examination of stereotypes and misconceptions surrounding the Roma as both victims and perpetrators of crime, particularly trafficking, form an important part of the novel's attempt to raise reader awareness of TCT.

---

[7] These representations reflect media reports on domestic trafficking of vulnerable girls in northern England; see Perraudin (2016).

[8] For other portrayals of children transnationally trafficked for sexual abuse purposes, see Craig (2012) and Mistry (2016).

Girl is mainly preoccupied with transnational child sex trafficking; however, the text gives a realistic depiction of TCT without sensationalising the sexual aspect, in contrast to some crime novels featuring TCT plot-lines, such as Craig's *Buckingham Palace Blues* which seems to exaggerate the crime for shock effect, by having a young abused trafficked girl ask a police man "'We fuck now?'" (Craig, 2012, p. 13). *Girl* is less sensational-ist in its description of the traumatic effect on TCT victims of the sexual abuse they are subjected to (Riches, 2016, Part 1, Chap. 16). Riches' subtly harrowing portrayal of a distressed young, trafficked boy demon-strating to police the sexual abuse he was subjected to through the use of dolls, rather than through verbal evidence, reflects Bloom's recognition that "[s]ince a child's capacity for verbalization is just developing, their ability to put their traumatic experience into words is particularly difficult" (1999, p. 6). Through such descriptions, *Girl* demonstrates that language barriers for transnationally trafficked young children serve as an additional obstacle to adequately addressing and treating the victim's trauma. The novel draws a parallel between reports of TCT in the news media, and the reality encountered by its detective characters, describing one place where trafficked children are held as, "the basement of a semi-derelict Berlin townhouse where the stuff of nightmarish news reports was reality" (Riches, 2016, Part 3, Chap. 44). Alluding to media-demonised male pae-dophiles from Britain and Europe, *Girl* maintains the link established throughout the novel between masculinity, TCT and sexual abuse:

> No Joseph Fritzl or Fred West had stood guard, yet this situation had seemed so far worse to Piet: missing children, at the mercy of not one psy-chopath but an entire network of traffickers and abusers that saw young lives only as commodities to be exploited and monetised. (Riches, 2016, Part 3, Chap. 44)

Breaking down the boundary between fiction and reality in its references to vilified and infamous real-life child abusers, *Girl* suggests not only that media reports shape public perceptions of human trafficking, but, some-what problematically, that these representations are reflective of the reality of TCT.

Girl's complicated TCT plot reflects the point made by Conradi that "[t]rafficking in children is abetted by a number of political, economic and social factors" (2013, p. 1211), outlining the complex factors that result in parents selling their children to traffickers, and individuals abducting children for personal gain (2013, p. 1211). In contrast, the novel's other child trafficking plot, the abduction of two children from an affluent family, draws on a less common form of child trafficking, according to Rogers (2012). The focus in *Girl* on young children as victims of child sex trafficking reflects the news media focus on youth (Gregoriou & Ras, 2018), to some extent perpetuating established stereotypes about TCT, and echoing the idea of 'moral panic' in relation to TCT discussed by Cree et al. (2014). Through its use of British and European settings, the novel portrays TCT as an international crime involving organisations and gangs led by stereotypical ruthless and brutal traffickers (a feature also commented on by Moore & Goldberg, 2015, p. 21). *Girl* reflects the point made by Fussey and Rawlinson that "trafficking of children for sexual exploitation is very much part of the 'headline space' occupied by sex trafficking" (2017, p. 45). The novel occupies this "headline space" in its preoccupation with sex trafficking; however, its somewhat cluttered plotline prevents the reader from gaining a deeper, more nuanced understanding of child trafficking and the experiences of victims, or how to break the cycle of TCT.

HARRAGA AND DOMESTIC NOIR

Dugdall's *Nowhere Girl* (2015) uses the crime fiction subgenre of domestic noir[9] to portray trafficking of girls and young females from the Global South by means of *harraga* to Western European homes for purposes of forced labour and sexual exploitation (Dunning, n.d.). Set in Luxemburg and Algeria, the novel also depicts the disappearance in Luxemburg of Ellie, a 16-year-old British girl, whose mother has arranged for her to be kidnapped at a funfair to teach her a lesson (Dugdall, 2015, p. 246), and the efforts by ex-probation officer Cate Atkins to find the girl. The novel is told through multiple narrative perspectives, including those of the trafficked girls. *Nowhere Girl* portrays the pervasiveness of child trafficking and the invisibility of modern slavery in everyday life, using the child kidnapping plotline alongside a depiction of TCT and modern slavery. Both plotlines explore the role of parents and families in child trafficking (May, 2016).

[9] Crouch (2013) on domestic noir: "it takes place primarily in homes and workplaces, concerns itself largely (but not exclusively) with the female experience [...] and takes as its base a broadly feminist view that the domestic sphere is a challenging and sometimes dangerous prospect for its inhabitants."

Dugdall's portrayal reflects recent attention to human trafficking in Luxemburg. In a 2017 report, the President of the consulting commission on human rights called for greater awareness of the prevalence of human trafficking in the country, stating the country needs "awareness-raising about the types of human trafficking that exist among the wider public, hospital staff, social offices and teachers" (Bauldry, 2017).

The TCT plot in *Nowhere Girl* is based around the phenomenon of *harraga*, a term used to describe illegal immigrants from North Africa who have burned their personal documents in order to prevent identification by European authorities, "literally burn[ing] down social, cultural and familial identities" (Beneduce, 2008, p. 513; Abderrezak, 2016, p. 68). Dugdall's detailed depiction of the issue of *harraga*, and the social, cultural, and religious factors that give rise to it, makes the representation of human trafficking authentic and historically and culturally accurate. Her research into *harraga* goes beyond a superficial or sensationalised treatment and adds an important realistic dimension. *Nowhere Girl* portrays *harraga* through the depiction of the TCT of a young teenage girl, Amina, from her home in a poor Algerian village to Luxemburg. Through Amina's story, the reader learns about the cultural and religious problems that impact on families and communities in the Global South, leading to *harraga*. Amina's family is torn apart by religious conflict and patriarchal dominance, leading to her mother sending her daughter away to improve her life chances and to give her an education (Dugdall, 2015, pp. 26–27).[10] Amina is trafficked by a local Algerian man called "Uncle Jak", who lives in Europe but returns to the village twice a year with his truck to take children away (i.e., to traffick them), under the auspices of offering them a better life (Dugdall, 2015, pp. 28–29). The novel describes the financial and human cost for the family of deciding to send Amina to Europe: "The cost of *harraga* had been great. Omi had sold the vineyard [...] It was their only asset, sold secretly and quickly" (Dugdall, 2015, p. 79). The book also follows a 19-year-old woman called Jodie, who has also used *harraga* to travel to Europe with Amina, but who ends up being forced into prostitution. The novel's title, "Nowhere Girl", alludes to the invisibility of the trafficked girls from the police and authorities. Their existence without identity papers through *harraga*, enforced by

[10] Fox (2016) discusses the impact of religious intolerance, among a number of other factors, affecting what she calls "constructions of society and education." (pp. 57–58). See also Manian (2010).

trafficking, reflects a social division between those who are visible, and those who are not, that is, those who are "nowhere". By exploring the TCT victim's experience through Amina's perspective, *Nowhere Girl* renders visible the emotional and physical trauma experienced by victims. The treatment of TCT in Dugdall is well-contextualised, and the novel makes an important contribution to knowledge for readers and researchers of crime fiction, in its examination of *harraga*, and its effects and implications.

Amina and Jodie's trafficking narratives draw on stereotypical modes of female exploitation, such as nail bar work and sexual abuse (Pearce et al., 2013, p. 31).[11] Although both girls live together with an Algerian family in Luxemburg, descriptions of their living conditions clearly signal their slave status within the family. They are forbidden to go out, their sleeping arrangements are poor, the door to their dingy bedroom is locked from the outside, they are both given drugs every day (Dugdall, 2015, p. 138) and they are deprived of agency.[12] Amina is made to work in a nail bar, whereas Jodie is exploited sexually (Dugdall, 2015, p. 159). Damaged by sexual exploitation, Jodie later breaks down and tells Amina:

> They didn't bring us here to help us better ourselves. We are here to be used up, our beauty and our bodies [...] *Harraga* is a factory, and we girls are what it produces. But we are broken goods, and I am the first to break. When I am all used up, you will be next. (Dugdall, 2015, p. 227)

This critique of *harraga* and the illusion that it can lead to a better life, instead resulting in exploitation and slavery of trafficked females, is important in the novel's critical examination of TCT. Rather than offer freedom and opportunity in Europe, *harraga* seals the females' fate as powerless victims, "nowhere girls".

Nowhere Girl offers only a partial resolution of its trafficking plot. Whereas the novel provides rescue and a closure for the kidnapped white Western European Ellie, the two female trafficking victims from the Global South, Jodie and Amina, are abandoned in the plot with only a perfunctory rescue. The TCT victim, Amina, is left at a hospital in the care of the family that enslaved her, and Jodie is promised "a place to stay and an

[11] See also Craig (2012) and Mistry (2016) for representation of TCT for sexual exploitation purposes.
[12] See also Gangmasters (n.d.), "Spot the Signs".

allowance" (Dugdall, 2015, p. 254). No further mention is made of how the authorities might assist them in their recovery from trauma, or whether they will be reunited with their families. Nor is there a sense of acknowledgement that Amina is a child and therefore extremely vulnerable, simply left with the family who have previously exploited her. *Nowhere Girl* reflects the failure of crime fiction to portray what happens "after"—the crime is solved and order is restored, but at the expense of the victim whose story fades into insignificance. This silence mirrors real-life TCT cases, as reported by Bulman who states that, in Britain, "child slavery victims are deprived of specialised support, pushing them back into abuse" (2017b).

Organ Trafficking

Danish authors Kaaberbøl and Friis' *The Boy in the Suitcase* (2008, 2011)[13] focuses on various forms of TCT, including organ harvesting, illegal adoption, and sex trafficking.[14] *Boy* depicts human trafficking as a social and cultural problem that affects individuals and families profoundly, and promotes a nuanced portrayal of TCT through a multiple character perspective.[15] Set in Denmark, Lithuania, and Eastern Europe, the novel uses its organ trafficking plot to expose the exploitation of former Eastern Bloc countries and their resources by the West following the fall of the Berlin Wall (Stewart, 2016; see also Meyer, 2006). *Boy* follows Nina, the female investigator character and Red Cross nurse in a contemporary Danish society marked by social division, crime, and conflict. Through its quest motif and narrative structure, *Boy* creates a complex portrayal of TCT, reflecting how "a growing number of distinguished Danish crime novels are now exposing social issues like immigration-related tensions, drug usage, organized crime, human trafficking, and disruptions of family life, all symptoms of social disorder" (Brunsdale, 2016, "Denmark"). The problems in the Danish welfare society, including human trafficking, are explicitly referred to in the novel through Nina's response to the apathy of her fellow Danes: "if only she would let herself believe what no one else

[13] From here on referred to as *Boy*.
[14] See also McGilloway's (2013) representation of child trafficking for illegal adoption purposes.
[15] In *Invisible Murder* (2010; 2012), Kaaberbøl and Friis treat the subject of the trafficking of dangerous substances and Roma adults and children.

seemed to have any trouble believing: that Denmark was a safe haven for the broken human lives that washed up on its shores" (Kaaberbøl & Friis, 2011, p. 204). This social-realist critique engenders a compelling analysis of TCT but falls back on narrative patterns of heroic rescue and innocent victims which are often reproduced in TCT narratives, according to Fussey and Rawlinson (2017, p. 52).

Boy educates readers about the anguish and human suffering caused by TCT. This novel also features an abduction plot, alongside descriptions of other forms of exploitation such as female sex trafficking. *Boy* portrays a Lithuanian single mother Sigita, whose three-year-old son Mikas is taken from her at a playground. She later wakes up in hospital, having been drugged and beaten up by Mikas' kidnappers. Sigita traces Mikas to Denmark, by tracking down accomplices in the TCT ring, and travels there to reclaim her son. Meanwhile, Nina is given a key by an acquaintance to a locker at Copenhagen train station, where she finds Mikas alive inside a suitcase in the locker. The title of *Boy* alludes to the mode of transportation used in the novel for TCT, anticipating a TCT case from 2015, in which an eight-year-old boy from the Ivory Coast was trafficked to Spain inside a suitcase (Kassam, 2015). *Boy*'s story follows her quest to discover the little boy's identity, while being hunted by Jucas, the trafficker who kidnapped Mikas, as well as Sigita. Jucas' mission is to bring the boy he has trafficked to a wealthy Danish couple whose adopted son is suffering from kidney failure and urgently needs a compatible transplant in exchange for a large sum of money. Mikas is compatible, because the sick boy is his older brother, illegally adopted at birth in Lithuania by the Danish couple when Sigita was only fifteen. *Boy*'s organ trafficking plot thus revolves around a critique of the acquisition of organs for the privileged wealthy in Western Europe through criminal means such as TCT from former Eastern Bloc countries such as Lithuania (Stewart, 2016).

Mikas' mother Sigita is the focus in the narrative for an exploration of maternal affect and the mother without her child (Hansen, 1997).[16] The novel's inclusion of the portrayal of a mother whose child has been trafficked, allows for an examination of an area of trafficking commonly absent from debates and representations around this crime—namely maternal experience. *Boy*'s representation of the mother's abjection

[16] Dugdall's *Nowhere Girl* also includes maternal perspectives in its trafficking narrative, in the form of confessional-tone letters written to Ellie, the kidnapped daughter from Bridget, the guilt-ridden mother who arranged it.

encourages the reader to empathise with the mother and her loss and confront the trafficked child's trauma.[17] Including these important yet frequently omitted dimensions contributes to *Boy*'s nuanced representation of TCT. *Boy* describes Mikas' traumatised behaviour, screaming uncontrollably and urinating on the floor with fear (Kaaberbøl & Friis, 2011, pp. 225–257), reflecting what Bloom calls "engraving of trauma": "When we are overwhelmed with fear, we lose the capacity for speech, we lose the capacity to put words to our experience" (1999, p. 5). This depiction and other portrayals in the novel of Mikas give the reader an insight into the harmful effects of trauma on trafficked children, through *Boy*'s realistic portrayals of traumatised behaviours and responses.[18] The significance of this type of depiction is highlighted by Vickroy who commends, "the capacity of trauma in literature to engage the reader's empathy by closely examining the personal and community contexts of trauma and its psychological ramifications" (2014, p. 148). As part of the novel's complex representation of TCT, the reader also learns about Jucas, the novel's brutal trafficker whose character reflects the stereotypically thuggish trafficking villain described by Moore and Goldberg (2015, p. 21). Having been sexually abused in an orphanage (Kaaberbøl & Friis, 2011, p. 265), Jucas, in turn, brutalises others, as his reflections on torturing his victims reveal (Kaaberbøl & Friis, 2011, p. 157). Jucas' view of Mikas that, "the kid was currency" (Kaaberbøl & Friis, 2011, p. 208) further demonstrates how children are objectified and commodified through TCT trafficking.

Boy depicts how Nina is affected in her personal and professional life by her demanding and often harrowing work with refugees and human trafficking victims. Her reflections on the difficulties of her work serve the purpose of educating the reader regarding human trafficking, as she considers TCT, and the brutality of the people behind it, as well as the indifference of the general population: "the real beauty of it all for the cynical exploiters was that ordinary people didn't care" (Kaaberbøl & Friis, p. 213). Nina's work gives her an awareness of the ways in which children are exploited and abused, such as children forced by traffickers to beg and steal, sold by parents, instructed to escape from refugee centres and authorities (Kaaberbøl & Friis, 2011, p. 214). Like *Girl* and *Nowhere Girl*, *Boy* portrays the impact of social inequality on individual victims

---

[17] See Hansen's (1997) examination of maternal loss of children.
[18] See Rafferty (2008) on the emotional and psychological damage caused to trafficked children.

vulnerable to opportunistic crime, but also shows how traffickers may themselves be impacted on by these environments and acting out of economic necessity. *Boy*'s quest-driven rescue narrative resolves its TCT plot by returning Mikas to his mother; however, both Sigita and Mikas are dropped from the story following his return. *Boy*'s quest narrative is constructed around central questions of identity and belonging: the quest to discover the identity of the little boy and to keep him safe from traffickers, to reunite him with his mother and return him to where he belongs. These are narrative resolutions with which readers can identify emotionally; but although this affective dimension is important, it cannot mask the gap in *Boy*'s trafficking narrative: the question of what happens to the TCT victim and his family after the rescue and what support (if any) they receive.

CHILD SOLDIERS AND VICTIMS

Swedish author Schepp's (2016) novel *Marked for Life*[19] uses crime fiction subgenres, such as the psychological novel and the police procedural,[20] to investigate the issue of child soldiers: children who have been trafficked transnationally and forcibly trained to fight, often being exposed to, and suffering the effects from, extreme violence (Child Recruitment and Use, n.d.). The theme of child soldiering is unusual in crime fiction, and Schepp's treatment of the theme makes her novel stand out from the other crime texts discussed earlier, and their predominant focus on child sex trafficking or individual child abductions. Commenting on child soldiering, Tiefenbrun states that: "The use and abduction of child soldiers is an international crime and a heinous human rights violation that is caught in the intersection of four different but related areas of the law: children's rights, slavery, human trafficking, and exploitative child labor" (2007, p. 434). Child soldiers tend to be recruited in areas of armed conflict involving warlords, such as Africa and Asia (Mapp, 2010, p. 72); however, Schepp's novel transposes this particular TCT crime into a Swedish setting

---

[19] From here on referred to as *Marked*.

[20] The psychological crime novel focuses on inner dimensions, exploring the thoughts and reflections of characters, including experiences of, and responses to, trauma. The police procedural depicts the workings of a police force in their crime solving efforts, focusing on individual police characters as well as on their team work. See also Worthington (2011).

in order to examine its devastating effect on individuals, families, and communities.

Set in Sweden, *Marked* opens with the murder of the head of the migration board, an event that forces together the two main threads in the narrative, namely the use of child soldiers and the female protagonist, public prosecutor Jana Berzelius. It transpires during the police investigation that the aforementioned murder was committed by a child soldier who is later found dead. *Marked* uses the interspersed harrowing flashbacks of a young girl who is being trafficked from Chile with her parents inside a container alongside a number of other families, having been promised a bright future in Europe (Schepp, 2016, p. 22). However, the girl's graphic memories of the scene reveal that all the adults in the container are killed on arrival by the traffickers, and the children taken away, beaten, drugged, and forcibly trained to become child soldiers. The girl is renamed Ker by the traffickers as part of a brutal training regime which involves getting her addicted to drugs and forcing her to fight the other children to the death. Making child soldiers dependent on hard drugs is a strategy for control, as Tiefenbrun points out (2007, p. 478). The trafficker, whom Ker only knows as "the man with the scar", carves the children's soldier names into their necks, to establish their new identities which he controls (Schepp, 2016, p. 89). Only later does the reader make the connection between Jana and Ker, the girl who has been trafficked and is being exploited as a child soldier, through the description of the characteristic scar on Jana's neck, a strategy which also assists the reader in understanding Jana's trauma. Jana's recurring nightmares and violent responses reflect Vickroy's assertion that "[f]iction that depicts trauma incorporates varied responses and survival behaviours within the characterization of survivors" (2014, p. 130). Through the character of Jana/Ker, *Marked* engenders the reader's engagement with the trauma suffered by trafficked child soldiers and reconsideration of their assumptions about children and innocence (see also Fussey & Rawlinson, 2017).

Through her realist portrayal, Schepp calls attention to the brutal strategies used to transform a child into a slave and a soldier, themes which she states are common to Nordic Noir (Zander, 2016). As in *Boy*, Schepp's focus on TCT reflects a trend in Scandinavian crime fiction to investigate controversial topics, reflecting a critical awareness of social and cultural failings such as "crime and terrorism; domestic violence; drug and alcohol abuse; human trafficking; local and international gang activity" (Brunsdale, 2016, "Introduction"). Schepp has spoken in a "Shots: Crime and Thriller

Ezine" feature about human trafficking and child soldiering, stating that "this actually happens in Sweden today [...] Adults and children disappear, are kidnapped, are taken away and are forced into a life of prostitution or slavery. Human traffickers profit on people in peril" (Schepp, n.d.). Child soldiering has been associated mainly with African and Middle Eastern countries in recent decades (Mapp, 2010, p. 69); however, Schepp's use of this form of human trafficking in a Swedish context raises reader awareness and draws attention to the global impact of child soldiering.

By depicting the brutalisation of Jana/Ker during her combat training, and the life-long damaging impact on her as an adult, *Marked* examines the emotional and psychological trauma experienced by child soldiers. These problems are also discussed by Tiefenbrun who states that child soldiers "feel guilty because they have survived [...] The children have lost their autonomy and self-control" (2007, p. 478). As an adult, Jana remains haunted by memories and sounds which return to torment her in her dreams. She wants to unlock the trauma but cannot find the key:

> She had experienced the same dream for as long as she could remember. It was always the same images. It irritated her that she didn't understand what the dream meant. She had turned, twisted and analyzed all the symbols each time she fell victim to it. (Schepp, 2016, p. 46)

These descriptions echo Vickroy's explanation of the strategies used in fiction to represent traumatised individuals: "Through familiar literary elements trauma fiction creates constructs of that experience with proto-typically imagined situations and symptoms, metaphoric dreams, death imagery, and narrative styles that mimic such experience, for example, fragmented thoughts, dissociative outlook, de-contextualized visualization, etc."(2014, p. 138) When Jana sees a dead boy (a child soldier) bearing evidence of brutal physical abuse, with a name carved into his neck similar to hers, her recognition of the sign and extreme reaction reflect the severity of the trauma she has suffered, "the ground began to rock beneath her feet. She gripped the edge of the table with both hands so as not to fall" (Schepp, 2016, p. 135). This and other descriptions of Jana's trauma allow the reader to understand the affective impact of TCT and to recognise it as a crime against the individual child. At the end of the novel, Jana confronts Papa, the man with the scar who trafficked her and brutalised her. In a bid to maintain his control over her, he tells her that she was just an "illegal kid", "meaningless" (Schepp, 2016, p. 359), and explains that

"In many countries there are young people who are deliberately recruited, trained and used in armed forces. I do the same here" (Schepp, 2016, pp. 361–362). Although the novel does not bring a resolution for Jana, it illustrates in graphic ways the horrors of child soldiering, and the ruthlessness of those involved in TCT, but also the incredible resilience and courage of children who have survived severe trauma.

Walters' *The Cellar* (2015) specifically uses the trafficked child's perspective to explore the harrowing effects of TCT, forced labour, and sexual abuse, and the violent feelings and responses this abuse may generate in the victim. In Walters' novel, the female protagonist Muna has been fraudulently obtained from a Nigerian orphanage at age 8 by the Songolis, an African family who then trafficked her to Britain. Here, they keep her as a domestic slave, locked away, subjected to physical punishment and beatings, and sexual abuse by the father of the family. The dark cellar, in which she is imprisoned at night, also the site of her sexual abuse, becomes a symbolic space marking the invisibility and silence of the trafficking victim.[21] The novel depicts how Muna, now aged 14, starts avenging herself on the Songoli family, whose members disappear one by one. *The Cellar* problematises the focus in the conventional trafficking narrative on rescue, in its rejection of a happy ending and restoration of normality for the child victim. Instead, Walters' represents TCT as an invisible scourge that undermines the family unit and haunts affluent Western societies. *The Cellar* uses the motif of captivity as a central motif, with the cellar itself as a symbol of that captivity and the trauma inflicted through TCT. Drawing on the psychological thriller and domestic noir, *The Cellar* places the patriarchal family at the heart of its TCT portrayal, interrogating its damaging power dynamics and resulting taboo feelings of rage in the child victim. This novel provides a clear example of how, as Vickroy states, "[f]iction provides readers with a wealth of thick description of the conditions and characteristics of traumatic experience" (2014, p. 137). Muna's rage transforms the cellar, from a space where she was abused, to the locus for her deadly revenge. However, her rage is also symptomatic of a traumatised child's cry for help, echoing Caruth's assertion regarding trauma that: "It is this plea by an other who is asking to be seen and heard, this call by which the other commands us to awaken" (1996, p. 9). As in *Marked*, these compelling but appalling representations of trafficked girls,

---

[21] This text is discussed in more detail in Gregoriou and Beyer, 2019.

their rage and capacity for extreme violence illustrate with perhaps the greatest clarity the devastation caused by trafficking. Even in crime fiction, a genre driven by representations of violence and transgression, these shocking portrayals make for difficult reading.

Works like those by Schepp, Walters, and Dugdall appear to be the exception in the growing body of popular literature portraying human trafficking, in their sustained narrative focus on the trafficked child's experience and trauma. In crime fiction generally, victims are seldom given the main voice and narrative perspective, and this silence or absence contributes to the stereotypical construction of victimhood as devoid of agency. Such narrative erasure extends to representations of human trafficking and its victims, where specifically children's perspectives tend to be absent from fictional depictions of this crime. However, in the novels by Schepp, Walters, and Dugdall, it is the victims' characters and stories that are the most compelling and emotionally engaging aspects of the crime plot. Their TCT narratives are not determined by ideas of innocence or rescue, but instead by individual self-preservation and courage. By foregrounding TCT characters within the narratives and giving these victims presence and agency within the stories, these novels contribute to producing a more nuanced picture of trafficking and victimhood, one which seeks to challenge stereotypes, but also conveys the victim's feelings of violence, desire for revenge, and hatred.

Conclusion: The Politics of Representing TCT in Crime Fiction

The representation in crime fiction of TCT, the child victims and their families, has rarely received critical attention as a subject in its own right. This oversight detracts from the way in which literature contributes to current debates around the relationship between Western Europe, the former Eastern Bloc and the Global South, which are played out in human trafficking narratives. However, as we have seen, crime fiction novels feature complex storylines about TCT, some of which present child victims at the centre of the narrative. Using a range of thematic and textual means, the texts examined in this chapter explore the cultural narratives that dominate how readers perceive children, and the foundational texts with their patterns of heroic rescue which tend to dominate their portrayal, and contribute to affecting and shaping contemporary cultural, social, and political responses to TCT (Fussey & Rawlinson, 2017, p. 55). These crime novels here thus implicitly or explicitly engage in public and private debates around human trafficking (Dugdall; Kaaberbøl & Friis; Schepp; Walters), and contribute vitally to a wider understanding of academic research into human trafficking (Riches) (see also Bickford, 2012). Through its popular outreach, crime fiction thus has the potential to affect popular perceptions of human trafficking.

Assessing the gender political dimensions of the TCT portrayal in the novels examined, we have seen that certain stereotypes prevail, and that these are particularly pronounced in the portrayal of traffickers. Human traffickers tended to be male, particularly when their actions were associated with violence and brutality, whereas females typically played an accomplice role, but were rarely in charge of trafficking operations (Riches; Dugdall; Kaaberbøl & Friis; Schepp). This conventional gender role distribution can also be observed in representations of trafficking victims in popular culture which concentrate on female sex trafficking, thereby "oversimplify[ing] dynamics of trafficking and global migration, [and] recreat[ing] damaging stereotypes about victims" (Kinney, 2014, p. 104). In the novels examined here, the child victims portrayed are of both genders, suggesting that where TCT depiction in crime fiction is concerned, gender roles are less stereotypically conceived than in media reportage, for example, which tends to focus on adult (although young) female victims of sex trafficking (Gregoriou & Ras, 2018). Likewise, the theme of the family features prominently in the plot of several of these crime fictions, reflecting a preoccupation with the theme of identity, but also drawing attention to the complex role family plays in TCT. Cree et al. argue that, "contemporary trafficking stories highlight the uncaring parents who sell children into servitude and the cruel 'people traffickers' who exploit them financially and sexually" (2014, p. 431). The crime fictions discussed here problematise the role and agency of parents in TCT, especially Dugdall; Kaaberbøl and Friis, raising questions surrounding responsibility and neglect which are key to constructions of gender and parenting (see also Moore & Goldberg, 2015, pp. 22–23).

The narrative patterns and moral themes utilised in crime fiction highlight the already heightened and exaggerated stereotypes often at play in cultural and media representations of human trafficking. These stereotypes frequently form part of the TCT narrative which, according to Cree et al., is often construed as:

a morality tale of 'goodies' (the innocent child victims) [...], 'baddies' (the cruel perpetrators, often portrayed as 'foreigners') and 'saviours' (the police

officers, social workers, politicians, and NGO workers who bring this issue
to the public's attention and 'save' children from harm. (Cree et al., 2014,
p. 429, also cited in Fussey and Rawlinson, 2017, p. 54)

According to Fussey and Rawlinson, such narratives result in TCT crimes
"occup[ying] headlines and print space" (2017, p. 54), which, however,
do not result in "prosecutions and criminal justice interventions" (2016,
p. 45). As stereotypical representations of trafficked children are perpetuated through the dominant narrative of rescue which reinforce trafficking
clichés, these representations do not address the cycle of trafficking or
fundamentally change how victims are seen. Crime fiction texts rarely tell
the story of what happens to victims after the rescue. This erasure from
trafficking narratives of the aftermath of crime and the victim's experience
extends to real life, too, as Bulman explains: "Victims of slavery and human
trafficking 'abandoned' as soon as they are identified. Trafficked victims
who escape sexual exploitation and domestic servitude face 'sharp cliff
edge' as no provisions are systematically put in place to assist their recovery" (2017a; Bokhari, 2008). However, in terms of narrative function, the
crime fictions examined here attempt at least a partial restoration of order
and justice for victims, a central purpose of the genre. Along with suspense
and problem-solving, these are narrative elements that appeal to readers
and enable them to cope with the otherwise bleak representations of violence and harm in TCT.

This chapter has argued that crime fiction has the capacity to put a
human face to TCT, through nuanced portrayals created through political
use of literary language and form, thus underlining the significance of literary representation. As Nestingen states, contemporary crime fiction
presents "stories [that] use crime to engage with debates over individual-
ism, collective claims, and the status of national homogeneity, gender, and
transnational relations" (2008, p. 14). Ruivo reminds us that trafficking
victims are already marginalised or disregarded within their societies,
because of their gender, age, social status, and lack of authority (2015,
p. 22). The power and influence of representation is undeniable, as
Andrijasevic and Mai (2016) state, particularly when it comes to "understanding the historical, cultural and political specificity of the figure of the
[trafficking] victim". Crime fiction authors are responding to the pressing
call for more authentic representations of TCT, a call echoed by Gregoriou
and Ras (2018) in relation to media representations of human trafficking,
and for more efforts to be made in order to support victims. Through its

compelling representations and insistence on their presence, crime fiction plays an significant role in negating the invisibility and abandonment of TCT victims.

REFERENCES

Abderrezak, H. (2016). *Ex-centric migrations: Europe and the Maghreb in Mediterranean cinema, literature, and music.* Indiana: Indiana University Press.

Andrijasevic, R., & Mai, N. (2016). Editorial: Trafficking (in) representations: Understanding the recurring appeal of victimhood and slavery in neoliberal times. *Anti-Trafficking Review,* (7). Retrieved December 8, 2017, from http://www.antitraffickingreview.org/index.php/atrjournal/issue/view/15

Bauldry, J. (2017, March 16). Lux. Is failing human trafficking victims. *Delano.* Retrieved November 9, 2017, from http://delano.lu/d/detail/news/lux-failing-human-trafficking-victims/139863

Beneduce, R. (2008). Undocumented bodies, burned identities: Refugees, sans papiers, harraga when things fall apart. *Social Science Information, 47*(4), 505–527.

Bickford, D. M. (2010). Novels, public policy and anti-trafficking efforts. In *Second Annual Interdisciplinary Conference on Human Trafficking,* 2010. Paper 5, pp. 1–7. Retrieved December 13, 2017, from http://digitalcommons.unl.edu/humtrafconf2/5

Bickford, D. M. (2012). "We all like to think we've saved somebody": Sex trafficking in literature. *Journal of International Women's Studies, 13*(3), 127–136.

Bloom, S. L. (1999) "Trauma theory abbreviated." from *The final action plan: A coordinated community-based response to family violence.* Attorney General Mike Fisher's Task Force on Family Violence. Retrieved November 9, 2017, from http://sanctuaryweb.com/

Bokhari, F. (2008). Falling through the gaps: Safeguarding children trafficked into the UK. *Children and Society, 22,* 201–211.

Brunsdale, M. M. (2016). *Encyclopedia of Nordic crime fiction: Works and authors of Denmark, Finland, Norway and Sweden since 1967.* Jefferson: McFarland. Kindle.

Bulman, M. (2017a, May 21). Victims of slavery and human trafficking "abandoned" as soon as they are identified. *The Independent.* Retrieved September 28, 2017, from http://www.independent.co.uk/news/uk/home-news/human-trafficking-slavery-a7743816.html

Bulman, M. (2017b, October 13). Government urged to overhaul slavery policy as child victims slip back into exploitation after being rescued. *The Independent.*

Retrieved November 9, 2017, from http://www.independent.co.uk/news/uk/home-news/slavery-policy-child-victims-national-referral-mechanism-government-overhaul-exploitation-a7998656.html

Caruth, C. (1996). *Unclaimed experience: Trauma, narrative and history.* Baltimore, MD: Johns Hopkins University Press.

Child Recruitment and Use. (n.d.). Office of the special representative of the general secretary for children and armed conflict. *United Nations.* Retrieved November 9, 2017, from https://childrenandarmedconflict.un.org/effects-of-conflict/six-grave-violations/child-soldiers/

Craig, J. (2012). *Buckingham Palace blues.* London: Robinson. Kindle.

Cree, V. E., Clapton, G., & Smith, M. (2014). The presentation of child trafficking in the UK: An old and new moral panic? *British Journal of Social Work, 44*(2), 418–433.

Crouch, J. (2013). Genre bender. *Blog.* Retrieved December 17, 2017, from http://juliacrouch.co.uk/blog/genre-bender

Dearey, M. (2018). Who are the traffickers? A cultural criminological analysis of traffickers as represented in the Al Jazeera documentary series *Modern Slavery: A Twenty-First Century Evil.* In C. Gregoriou (Ed.), *Representations of transnational human trafficking: Present-day news media, true crime, and fiction.* Basingstoke: Palgrave.

Diamond, K. (2016, November 30). Marnie Riches and Katarina Diamond in conversation. *The Crime Readers' Association.* Retrieved September 28, 2017, from https://thecra.co.uk/marnie-riches-katerina-diamond-conversation/

Dodd, L. (2015). The crime novel as trauma fiction. Minding the gap: Writing across thresholds and fault lines papers. In *The refereed proceedings of the 19th conference of the Australasian Association of Writing Programs, 2014,* Wellington NZ. Retrieved November 9, 2017, from http://www.aawp.org.au/publications/minding-the-gap-writing-across-thresholds-and-fault-lines/

Dugdall, R. (2015). *Nowhere girl.* London: Legend Press.

Dunning, M. E. (n.d.). Nowhere girl by Ruth Dugdall. *Mari Illis Dunning.* Retrieved November 9, 2017, from https://mariellisdunning.cymru/book-reviews/nowhere-girl-by-ruth-dugdall/

Fox, C. (2016). Who is my neighbour? Unleashing our postcolonial consciousness. *The International Education Journal: Comparative Perspectives, 15*(3), 57–76.

Fussey, P., & Rawlinson, P. (2017). *Child trafficking in the EU: Policing and protecting Europe's most vulnerable.* Abingdon: Routledge.

Gangmasters & Labour Abuse Authority. (n.d.). Spot the signs. Retrieved November 9, 2017, from http://www.gla.gov.uk/who-we-are/modern-slavery/who-we-are-modern-slavery-spot-the-signs/

Gregoriou, C., & Beyer, C. (under consideration 2019). The transnational human trafficking victim in Minette Walters' *The Cellar.* A critical and stylistic analysis of the complexity of victim representation in crime fiction. In U. Tabbert &

J. Douthwaite (Eds.), *The linguistics of crime*. Cambridge: Cambridge University Press.

Gregoriou, C., & Ras, I. A. (2018). "Call for purge on the people traffickers": An investigation into British newspapers' representation of transnational human trafficking, 2000–2016. In C. Gregoriou (Ed.), *Representations of transnational human trafficking: Present-day news media, true crime, and fiction*. Basingstoke: Palgrave.

Hansen, E. T. (1997). *Mother without child: Contemporary fiction and the crisis of motherhood*. University of California Press.

Jacomella, C. (2010). Media and migrations: Press narrative and country politics in three European countries. *Reuters Institute Fellowship Paper*. Oxford: Oxford University. pp. 1–102. Retrieved December 19, 2017, from http://reutersinstitute. politics.ox.ac.uk/sites/default/files/research/files/Media%2520and%2520migrations%2520Press%2520narrative%2520and%2520country%2520politics%2520in%2520three%2520European%2520countries.pdf

Johnson, M. (2017). *Deadly game*. London: Orenda Books.

Jonsson, A. (2009). Introduction: Human trafficking and human security in the Baltic Sea region. In A. Jonsson (Ed.), *Human trafficking and human security* (pp. 1–9). Abingdon: Routledge.

Kaaberbøl, L., & Friis, A. (2008, 2011 Eng.transl.). *The boy in the suitcase*. New York: Soho. Kindle.

Kaaberbøl, L., & Friis, A. (2010, 2012 Eng.transl.). *Invisible murder*. New York: Soho. Kindle.

Kassam, A. (2015, May 8). X-ray scan at Spanish border finds child stashed inside suitcase. *The Guardian*. Retrieved November 9, 2017, from https://www.theguardian.com/world/2015/may/08/x-ray-scan-at-spanish-border-finds-child-stashed-inside-suitcase

Kelly, A., & Hodal, K. (2017, July 30). "Traffickers take all that makes you human": Faces of modern slavery—In pictures. *The Guardian*. Retrieved December 13, 2017, from https://www.theguardian.com/global-development/gallery/2017/jul/30/traffickers-take-all-makes-you-human-faces-modern-slavery-in-pictures

Kinney, E. (2014). Victims, villains, and valiant rescuers: Unpacking sociolegal constructions of human trafficking and crimmigration in popular culture. In M. J. Guia (Ed.), *The illegal business of human trafficking* (pp. 87–108) Cham: Springer.

Larsson, S. (2006, 2009). *The girl who played with fire*. London: MacLehose Press.

Manian, S. (2010). The wretched of the earth: Trafficking, the Maghreb, and Europe. In K. A. McCabe & S. Manian (Eds.), *Sex trafficking: A global perspective* (pp. 83–90). Plymouth: Lexington Books.

Mapp, S. C. (2010). *Global child welfare and well-being*. Oxford: University of Oxford Press.

May, R. (2016, May 28). 'Nowhere girl' by Ruth Dugdall. Promoting crime fiction by Lizzie Hayes. Retrieved November 9, 2017, from http://promotingcrime.blogspot.co.uk/2016/05/nowhere-girl-by-ruth-dugdall.html

McGilloway, B. (2013). *The stolen child*. London: Pan. Kindle.

Meyer, S. (2006). Trafficking in human organs in Europe: A myth or an actual threat? *European Journal of Crime, Criminal Law and Criminal Justice, 14*(2), 208–229.

Mistry, L. (2016). *Unquiet souls*. [Place of publication not identified]: Bloodhound Books.

Moore, A. S., & Goldberg, E. S. (2015). Victims, perpetrators and the limits of human rights discourse in post-Palermo fiction about sex trafficking. *The International Journal of Human Rights, 19*(1), 16–31.

Muždeka, N. (2018). Not all human trafficking is created equal: Transnational human trafficking in the UK and Serbian news media texts—Narratological and media studies approaches. In C. Gregoriou (Ed.), *Representations of transnational human trafficking: Present-day news media, true crime, and fiction*. Basingstoke: Palgrave.

Nestingen, A. (2008). *Crime and fantasy in Scandinavia: Fiction, film and social change*. Seattle: University of Washington Press.

Neville, S. (2011). *Stolen souls*. London: Harvell Secker.

Pearce, J. J., Hynes, P., & Bovarnick, S. (2013). *Trafficked young people: Breaking the wall of silence*. London: Routledge.

Perraudin, F. (2016, April 8). Rochdale grooming case: Nine men jailed for up to 25 years each. *The Guardian*. Retrieved December 15, 2017, from https://www.theguardian.com/uk-news/2016/apr/08/rochdale-grooming-case-10-men-sentenced-to-up-to-25-years-in-jail

Protocol to Prevent, Suppress and Punish Trafficking in Persons Especially Women and Children, supplementing the United Nations Convention against Transnational Organized Crime. (2000). United Nations Human Rights. Retrieved November 9, 2017, from http://www.ohchr.org/EN/ProfessionalInterest/Pages/ProtocolTraffickingInPersons.aspx

Rafferty, Y. (2008). The impact of trafficking on children: Psychological and social policy perspectives. *Child Development Perspectives, 2*(1), 13–18.

Riches, M. (2016). *The girl who walked in the shadows*. London: Harper Collins. Kindle.

Rogers, S. (2012, October 4). Child abduction in England & Wales: The key numbers. *The Guardian*. Retrieved December 14, 2017, from https://www.theguardian.com/news/datablog/2012/oct/04/child-abduction-statistics-england-wales

Ruivo, J. (2015). The fragilities of human trafficking victims. In M. J. Guia (Ed.), *The illegal business of human trafficking* (pp. 21–28). Cham: Springer.

Schepp, E. (2014; 2016). *Marked for life*. London: HQ. Kindle.

Schepp, E. (n.d.). The inspiration behind marked for life. *Shots: Crime & Thriller Ezine*. Retrieved November 9, 2017, from http://www.shotsmag.co.uk/feature_view.aspx?FEATURE_ID=344

Stewart, F. (2016). Der Frauenkrimi: Women's crime writing in German. In K. Hall (Ed.), *Crime fiction in German: Der Krimi* (European crime fictions). Cardiff: University of Wales Press. Kindle (Chapter 6).

Tiefenbrun, S. (2007). Child soldiers, slavery and the trafficking of children. *Fordham International Law Journal, 31*(2), 415–486.

Vickroy, L. (2014). Voices of survivors in contemporary fiction. In M. Balaev (Ed.), *Contemporary approaches in literary trauma theory* (pp. 130–151). London: Palgrave Macmillan.

Walters, M. (2015). *The cellar*. London: Harper Collins.

Worthington, H. (2011). *Key concepts in crime fiction*. Houndmills: Palgrave.

Zander, J. (2016, June 21). Nordic Noir is a reflection of modern Europe: Emelie Schepp & Joakim Zander discuss Scandinavian crime fiction as a mirror for evolving European societies. *Electric Lit*. Retrieved November 9, 2017, from https://electricliterature.com/nordic-noir-is-a-reflection-of-modern-europe-1508a07a5398

Who are the Traffickers? A Cultural Criminological Analysis of Traffickers as Represented in the Al Jazeera Documentary Series *Modern Slavery: A Twenty-first Century Evil*

Melissa Dearey

Abstract The aim of this chapter is to analyse and interrogate the identities of 'traffickers' as represented within a series of television documentaries on modern slavery. The chapter data set is a series of seven 25-minute documentaries entitled *Modern Slavery: A Twenty-first Century Evil* (2011) produced by Al Jazeera. Sections on trafficker identities and the usage of the term 'trafficker' within the different typologies represented in the documentary series are shown, that is, bridal, charcoal, prison, sex, food, child, bonded slavery/trafficking. These are represented within a complex geocultural televisual gaze (Al Jazeera English) upon the global north/west as ultimately the source of the slavery problem.

Keywords Cultural criminology • Documentary • Human trafficking • Modern slavery • Popular criminology • Trafficker • True crime

M. Dearey (✉)
University of Hull, Hull, UK
e-mail: m.dearey@hull.ac.uk

C. Gregoriou (ed.), *Representations of Transnational Human Trafficking*, https://doi.org/10.1007/978-3-319-78214-0_5

INTRODUCTION

The misery and abjection of human trafficking (henceforth HT) from the perspective of the victims has been, and continues to be, recognised and well documented in contemporary media representations of HT/modern slavery. This focus upon victims in this context is entirely justified for ethical, humanitarian, historical, economic, political, cultural, and legal-judicial reasons, and this is undisputed in this chapter. However, with a view to a better understanding and response to the plight of victims of HT, recently attention has begun to shift to those who traffic and/or enslave other human beings—commonly and henceforth referred to specifically in the context of human trafficking as 'traffickers' or more generically as 'perpetrators' (e.g., Gotch, 2016; Shen, 2016). Despite the slippages and complexities of the meanings of these two terms (also discussed in this book's Chap. 1), HT/modern slavery as an ontological-historical concept, global market activity, and also cultural-narrative trope is becoming more prominent and recognisable among audiences in the public sphere, not least as the result of the numerous fictional, factual, and hybrid 'factional' (Leishman & Mason, 2004) representations of it in the social and broadcast media and in the press.

The broader exposure of this and other forms of transnational organised crime[1] in the public sphere as a form of crime on the increase has contributed to its rise as a concern for law enforcement, politicians, and policy makers. Hence HT has also become a concern for criminology, whether from cultural, empirical, or policy making perspectives. As media representations of HT develop and expand, public interest and curiosity about it and what it is are invigorated. The market demand is for more, newer, and more revealing presentations of these narratives for the purposes of exposé or consumption, whether for information, public service, or entertainment, or a combination of these. As the criminologist and law professor Philip Rawlings (1998) argues, despite criminology's dismissive attitudes toward what he labels 'popular criminological' texts in the 'true crime' genre, these texts do shape public awareness and comprehension of crime and criminality, and subsequently impact governmental, legal, and

---

[1] 'Transnational organised crime' (or TOC) is itself a relatively new and in many ways also problematic term that has emerged into the public and global policy-making spheres in recent decades. With its 'apocalyptic' overtones in official and media discourses (Edwards & Gill, 2003, p, 1) it requires careful examination with respect to the processes of definition and its evolution from earlier designations of what came to be known as 'organised crime'.

security responses. It is justified for criminologists, therefore, to take such cultural narrative representations of crime more seriously as worthy datasets for analysis, not least to enhance the less than optimal status and influence of this discipline in the political and public spheres:

> Social historians have long recognised the value of popular crime literature in their work (Linebaugh 2006; Rawlings 1998); might there be something for academic criminologists too? Most important of all, it is popular writing about crime and criminals (fiction as well as fact) that has the greatest impact on people's understanding of crime and on criminal justice policy: Home Secretaries and their Shadows have never been noted for their interest in the views of academic criminologists (Rawlings, 1998: online).

Increasingly, attention is turning from victim accounts of HT to the traffickers themselves, in order to open new narrative and conceptual spaces for understanding and storytelling, and to shed light on their motives and the types of people they are in the representation of this type of crime. This chapter focuses upon the representation within HT narratives of trafficker identities in a particular television documentary series, namely *Modern Slavery: A Twenty-first Century Evil* (Al Jazeera, 2011, hereafter referred to as *S21*) as an example of 'true crime' or 'popular criminology' that portrays the identities and practices of traffickers. The chapter begins with a consideration of the methodological issues involved in conducting such a cultural criminological analysis of this dataset, comparing and relating my analysis and findings to other recent academic research articles focusing on trafficker identities in popular cultural and/ or popular criminological media texts. I then turn my attention to the definitions and narrative representations of traffickers in *S21*, analysing the differences and similarities between the narrative representations of traffickers in this documentary series that focus upon various types of HT. I find that the definition and identification of the 'trafficker' and where and how they operate in the international sphere are unclear, ambivalent, and unstable. The deployment and determination of the role or label 'trafficker' is significantly dependent upon the type of HT being discussed, the (perceived generic) gender and sexualities of the main population of victims, and the ethnic, racial, class, and national characteristics of those involved. The legal-judicial and cultural predisposition toward the individual (as opposed to collective groups) in isolating and exposing traffickers as inherently 'evil' also complicates and obfuscates the agencies (in both senses of the word to designate actors and institutions) involved in the trafficking of human beings. Programmes like *S21* demonstrate how changes to global governance and market economics that enable and exacerbate transnational organised crime as a distinctively modern form of evil HT taken together with the ordinary everyday discourses of victims and the prominence of presenter voices can affect the definition and assignment of the label 'trafficker'. While I concentrate my analysis on the seven episodes of *S21*, I will briefly compare my findings to 'trafficker' representations in a more recent Al Jazeera documentary *Britain's Modern Slave Trade* (Al Jazeera, 2016).

METHODOLOGY

The primary dataset for this chapter is comprised of the 2011 Al Jazeera produced documentary series *S21*, and secondarily the single episode documentary *Britain's Modern Slave Trade* (Al Jazeera, 2016). Like all texts examined in this book, the series was produced after the ratification of the 2000 Trafficking Protocol, commonly known as the Palermo Protocol. All book contributors recognise the salience of this statute, which provides a historical-political focus for each of our constituent contributions to the project and to this volume.

The broadcasting organisation Al Jazeera, also known as JSC or AJ, is a Doha-based state-funded broadcaster owned by the Al Jazeera Media Network. Founded in Qatar in 1996, Al Jazeera English was established in 2006. According to the report published in the widely respected journal *The Economist* (2017) attributed to the unnamed 'Cairo Correspondent', the emergence of Al Jazeera in the wake of the jettisoning of the 'irritatingly truthful' BBC Arabic language service from the Saudi operated satellite provided jobs for the previously BBC journalists, which the author accounts for the steeping of Al Jazeera investigative journalism in the early years at least in BBC culture and practice. However, with the growing conflict and political instability in the region, *The Economist* journalist indicates that this has changed, with AJ becoming more of a propaganda tool used to criticise Saudi Arabia and its allies, including the United Kingdom, the European Union and the United States of America. With respect to their factual documentary programming, AJ have and continue to operate something of an industry in the production of documentaries on modern slavery and HT focusing on the so called 'destination countries' of the global west and north, and this is indeed reflected in the direction of its criticisms toward the USA, Europe and the UK in *S21*.

All seven episodes of *S21* are presented by the Somali born former BBC presenter Rageh Omaar and was originally broadcast in 2011, at the height of the so called 'Arab Spring'. In 2016, the tenth anniversary of AJ English, the broadcaster produced and broadcast *Britain's Modern Slave Trade* (2016) focusing on the UK as a destination country and its role in the international sex, forced labour, and drugs trades. Reference to this other Al Jazeera documentaries will be considered alongside those presented in *S21*, but *S21* will be the predominant dataset and analytic focus of this chapter. As a dataset, this presents an interesting and previously over-looked perspective on these televisual 'true crime' or popular criminology narrative representations from the global south-east to north-west. This adds further dimensionality to the analysis and understanding of geopolitical and cultural discourses in the contemporary political, economic, and public and media spheres, as such geo-political semiotics become increasingly fractured, indeterminate, and unstable. How narrative representations are fashioned from the complex, fast-paced, and contradictory elements of HT in a global multi-media environment poses important questions in the shaping of public and policy knowledge of this and other forms of (trans)national organised crime. Who gets to say what, how, and why, about 'traffickers', and how this influences the construction and development of 'true crime' narratives are issues that will be addressed in light of this analysis in this chapter.

I next turn to the ontological frameworks and concepts with respect to narrative representations of human traffickers. As those responsible for causing harm to others (i.e., their victims), it is overwhelmingly *individuals* who are most commonly and primarily portrayed as 'traffickers' within conventional narrative representations of HT in media, although there is also evidence that the distinction between individuals and collective agencies when it comes to HT is breaking down (as exemplified in the later documentary *Britain's Modern Slave Trade*). The focus in *S21* on traffickers as individuals is consistent with the philosophical and onto-theological 'theodicy' type conceptualisation of narratives of evil. HT is represented in the title of *S21* as a 'twenty-first century evil', and this reflects a strong trend in modern philosophy with its focus on the construction of narrative based on the attribution of blame, guilt, and punishment to individual actors or agents who are deemed to be responsible moral agents for the suffering caused to victims (Dearey, 2014; Ricoeur & Pelauer, 1985). This rationalist modelling of the problem of evil renders good/evil and victims/perpetrators in a very dichotomous, oppositional, and 'black and white' way. This model has provided a template for the modern Western criminal justice system in the global north-west that endures to this day (Dearey, 2014). As is shown in documentaries like *S21*, such ontologies do not fit well with the lived realities of HT, nor do they (always) capture the evil, agency, or identities of traffickers, the suffering of the victims, or the fuller meanings of victim's discursive frameworks in describing their experiences of HT.

But the failure of 'fit' between theory and practice is not the only fault of traditional theodicy-type ontologies to HT. It is this almost myopic focus upon offenders from the rational-objectivist gaze of the state as adjudicators within the Western criminal justice system solely empowered to deal legitimately with crime. This has historically accounted for the *de facto* derogation or sideling of the victim from the judicial process, and also the disregard for the emotional dimensions and other more local impacts of crime. While the term 'victim' can be traced back to ancient times, and while victims have been the subject of criminological study since the 1920s and the era of the Chicago School, it was not until the 1950s that the social scientific study of victims—victimology—was formally established as a subfield of criminology, and even then, not until the 1970s that the needs and concerns of victims began to be taken seriously and to be catered for within the criminal justice system (Dussich, undated) and their voices prioritised in international law (Engdahl, 2002). Since the 1970s, the profile of the victim has dramatically risen in prominence, from the perspectives of popular and cultural representations of crime particularly, a substantive cultural shift that has fuelled many changes to legal-judicial discourses and practices. This swinging of the pendulum, if you will, to the focus upon the victim could be an unintentional contributing factor to why the identities of traffickers have been until recently somewhat less prominent in popular cultural representations of HT in true crime/documentary formats and fiction, all of which tend to highlight victims' experiences and testimonies. But even so, within victim testimonies such as those presented in *S21*, emerge potent diegetic[2] narratives of those they charge with responsibility for their victimisation—their *traffickers*. It is primarily from these testimonies featured in *S21*, and also presenter voiceover narratives, from which the data on traffickers are recovered.

---

[2] Diegesis is a form of narrative whereby characters comment upon and portray the thoughts and actions of other characters in their own stories or speech.

PREVIOUS RESEARCH

This analysis seeks to build upon a small corpus of similarly qualitative and interpretive analytic research of narrative representations of HT in popular cultural media. Two prominent recent examples are articles by Nicolas de Villiers (2016) and Sine Plambech (2016). In his study, de Villiers combines a feminist psychoanalytic film theory and theories of affect to deconstruct and critique a popular television miniseries and film documentary *Human Trafficking* (Lifetime Television, 2005). In his research, de Villiers identifies what he calls the 'hegemony of victimhood', that is, the ubiquity of the figure of the victim in these narratives that I alluded to in the previous section. To this he adds the significance of emotions and the body, particularly the 'affect of abolitionists' (de Villiers, 2016, p. 161) with reference to the strong emotional appeals by anti-prostitution campaigners in the construction of the televisual narrative series he analyses. According to de Villiers, these factors converge most prominently in the narrative conflation of women with HT victims—reflective of their concomitant lack of agency, and reliance upon a convergence of axial tropes relating to 'innocence', purity, exploitation, and the nationalist mythology of 'white slavery'. Though de Villiers considers HT solely within the European context, the white slavery narrative/mythology in popular cultural and media narrative representations of HT extends beyond Europe (see Namias, 1992). In her article, Plambech (2016) notes the prevalence of such 'one dimensional', distorted, and/or misleading dichotomised tropes that are foundational to many popular HT narratives of sex trafficking, exploring the reasons behind production decision-making processes in constructing these narratives, and the possibilities for breaking out of these reified tropes.

Building upon these analyses, in the next section, I interrogate how trafficker identities are defined and presented in *S21*, and how these definitions and representations differ not so much based on the identities or characteristics of the traffickers themselves (though these display some consistent regularities) but rather on what type of HT is being discussed in relation to the predominant gender of the *victims*. These differences within a television documentary series offer significant insights into the underlying presumptions and prevailing attitudes influencing current conceptualisations of HT generally, codified in the representation of traffickers. While my approach is similarly and intrinsically qualitative, in paying attention to the number of times and the narrative contexts in which the term 'trafficker' is used within and between the different episodes of *S21*, this analysis should be read alongside the more quantitative content analysis of use of terminologies in journalistic discourses about HT included in this volume.

Stigma and Deviance in *S21*

The term 'trafficker' is of relatively recent provenance, even newer than the also relatively current neologisms 'human trafficking' and 'modern slavery'. Though all of these phenomena are probably as old as human society itself, these terms are increasingly represented in the public sphere, in the media, and in academic and law enforcement arenas. But what do these terms mean, and how are they being used? How is the usage of a term like 'trafficker' within a television documentary series shaping understandings of this term, and wider perceptions of who human traffickers are? Do traffickers differ in their narrative construction and characterisation relative to the type of HT being presented, and if so, how, and why? The definition of 'trafficker' is far from clear, but how it is delineated within these documentaries in terms of how it is represented and used (or not) within HT narratives in the various episodes of *S21* is the focus of this section. As will be shown, the meanings and usages of this term are different in the context of different types of HT and in different (inter)national contexts. These differences appear to relate substantially to the gendering of the *victims* of HT, and also to the alignment of these forms of HT to other predominant or secondary ideological frames of HT as a form of modern slavery, which reference to discourses such as those of 'business', 'industry', 'natural disaster', 'state power', 'religious intolerance', 'love, marriage, and family life', and/or 'political dissent'.

Those involved in HT are being referred to as 'traffickers' or more generically as 'perpetrators' (e.g., Gotch, 2016; Shen, 2016). While the word 'perpetrator' is being used by some academics as a synonym or alternative word for 'trafficker', it is worth noting that neither are terms that are widely used in academic criminology, at least not in the UK. 'Perpetrator' is a word that is commonplace in many police procedural and true crime narratives—and has even been shortened to 'perp' in slang parlance in many popular television series—possibly more colloquially used by law enforcement officers and/or popular cultural representations of police procedural programmes in the USA. However, it is not a term that is formally or commonly used in criminology or law, which tend to use other terms like 'offender', 'suspect' or even 'criminal'. The use of slang terms, 'street' language, criminal/drug/gang terminologies or 'true crime' nomenclature in popular narrative representations of crime is significant here, as demonstrated in the popularity of the critically acclaimed HBO television series *The Wire* (2002–2008) in its representation of another type of (trans)national organised crime: the trade in illegal drugs. One of the most seminal and ground-breaking features of this series was the representation of the narrative in the vernacular dialogue of its characters, with an emphasis on the argot of (mainly) young black males and their communities and the language of 'the street'. This in turn led to the demand for audiences to learn and become conversant in these terms and discourses and the subsequent provision of numerous online and media dictionaries and glossaries to help viewers to understand what they were saying, with the expectation that this would reveal who the characters were, what they were doing and why, and that this provided audiences with real insights into crime and criminality in the illegal drugs trade. The effect was to give audiences a palpable sense that with this new language 'skill' that they had acquired came a new and informed knowledge and understanding of crime and also society, because they could 'speak' the lingo and understand the 'perps' on 'the street' and in the 'hoods'. Even if viewers had never seen or (knowingly) come into contact with an illicit Class A drug, addict, dealer, vice cop, or been to a housing project, even if they were not young, male, or black, they felt as if they knew the 'score' where any of these actors, agents, or their habitats or daily lives were concerned. This has been, and continues to be, an important and potent element of true crime and crime procedural fiction and 'faction' in terms of generating what are perceived by audiences to be meaningful narrative representations of crime. The use of language in these narratives conveys a real and abiding sense of knowledge about crime in the sense of how it happens, where, what the motivations are, who the criminals and victims are, and how they should be dealt with in the criminal justice system, primarily through how they talk, their vernacular functioning as a potent simulacrum for what is 'real'. Hence it is vital from the start to adopt a reflexive critical awareness with respect to the usage of language, images, sounds, and a constellation of different terminologies and tropes, and to pay attention to how and where these are derived and deployed within and between different expert and popular criminological epistemologies such as a true crime or factual television documentary. It is noteworthy here that in *S21*, the terms 'perpetrator', 'criminal', and 'offender' are not utilised by the programme makers as synonyms for 'trafficker'. Neither are the older terms 'slaveholder' or 'slaver' used, which is perhaps surprising, given the audio-visual tropes linking HT to transatlantic slavery embedded in the series. 'Trafficker' is used, but only in certain types of HT, and also only by certain speakers in specific contexts: most prominently, by the series presenter in voiceovers.

However, those who traffic human beings are certainly talked about, most authoritatively by their victims, and also by the traffickers themselves, the presenter, lawyers, and NGO workers—even if they don't use these words to identify them. I turn now to the terms used by those featured in *S21* to describe those who traffic human beings, or 'traffickers', and analyse how these narrative representations differ depending upon the types of HT victims and the speakers.

In all but two of the episodes of *S21*, 'criminals' are never mentioned. In the one instance that the term 'criminal' is mentioned, it is used to refer to the accusations of a trafficker against his *victims* in the episode on bonded/kiln slaves, in a voiceover by presenter Rageh Omaar:

> Some bonded labourers have sought to gain their freedom through the courts, only to find themselves accused by the kiln owners of criminal offenses. Without the means to defend themselves, they are frequently imprisoned. ('Bonded Slaves')

This statement underscores how powerful traffickers are in shaping and determining who is labelled as 'criminal' and the assignment of criminality, stigma, or deviance, displayed in their ability to marshal the powers of the state and its legal apparatus (or the threat of it) to intimidate and control their victims, and to prevent them from seeking justice or redress. In this episode, the presenter, other advocates, and NGO contributors consistently refer to those who traffic not as 'criminals' or indeed 'traffickers' but rather as 'owners':

> [Hina Jilani, Advocate:] When those who are repressing have ALL the access to state institutions, they have the power to use state institutions against the people they are oppressing. For instance, the police has [sic] always worked for the factory owners. The police has, at the behest of the factory owners, harassed and chased labourers when they have tried to escape. They have kept them in custody and tortured them, at the behest of *owners*. So it's not just the owners. It's the collusion of the state agencies that has made the power dynamics so much tilted in their favour. ('Bonded Slaves' [emphasis added])

There is however one episode of *S21* in which the term 'criminal' is widely used, but again never with reference to traffickers. As in the 'Bonded Slaves' episode where the term 'criminal' is used once, this is also with reference not to those who traffic, but to the victims of HT. These are some examples of how 'criminals' and 'criminalisation' are operationalised in HT in the laogai prison system in China which is the subject of 'Prison Slaves':

> For a year they tried to brainwash me, trying to force me to give up my practice of Falun Gong. They figured me out ... so they changed their strategy to force me to feel like a criminal ... because, according to their theory, a prisoner should be reformed through labour ... So they forced me to do slave labour. [Charles Lee who spent three years imprisoned for religious dissidence in the Chinese laogai]

But the role of the laogai prison system narrated in 'Prison Slaves' is not merely to criminalise victims:

> Chinese president say we want to see two products came from the labour camps. The number one product is the man who has been reformed, who is not going to fight against the Communist. Second product, the product, made by the man. [spoken by former prisoner and political activist Harry Wu]

In this episode, the narrative constructed is about the state using HT/modern slavery as a tactic to control, eliminate, and prevent political dissent and religious freedom, to enable 'reform' and additionally to generate money for the state from slave labour. Punishment through forced labour as a form of HT in this narrative has a multiple function. The state criminalises opposition, criticism, and dissent, forcing victims to conform to state ideology, thereby legitimising HT and absolving anyone involved in it on behalf of the state of any deviant or criminal label like 'trafficker'. This narrative is literally signposted for all those involved in the system to see. In one scene, Wu guides Rageh Omaar through an exhibition he has curated that includes photographs of the signs posted at the entrance to the camps photos. Entrants are presented with a sign that says 'Who are you? What is this place? Why are you here?' and another that states: 'You are a criminal. This is the laogai. You are here to reform through labour':

[Omaar voiceover:] Abigail was sent to Shenyang women's laogai Camp in northeast China. It holds an average 1,000 inmates, a mixture of drug addicts, criminals and religious dissidents. All are forced to work in its in-house factory.

This criminalisation has the effect of neutralising (inter)national concern or action to address the suffering of the victims. The narrative represents these 'criminals/prisoners' as those who deserve their 'punishment', and thereby fail to warrant protection or judicial intervention by this or other nation states, or the international polis. This is a state of denial (Cohen, 2001). Denial is a key theme of trafficker narratives across these documentaries. Where traffickers are made visible, they tend to deny their guilt, even to the point of claiming to be the victims themselves by default of being accused. Their implicit and sometimes explicit power to control the use of language pertaining to who is identified as criminal or deviant, and also to deflect their own deviance or criminality, is exposed in narratives of *S21*. This phenomenon is redolent of criminologist Lemert's (1967) influential thesis of primary and secondary deviance, whereby social elites are able to use their powerful status and capital to elide labels such as 'criminal' or 'trafficker', and to devolve these labels onto less powerful or lower status people, including their victims. The accusations of criminality (primary deviance) can be denied by social elites and this will be accepted by others in society, up to a point; it is when powerful elites exhaust their social capital in enforcing these narratives and others in society are no longer willing to accept their 'story' as valid that secondary deviance is operationalised. Then such elites are no longer seen as legitimate and their actions and identities are rejected and stigmatised. An integral part of this process is the creation of deviant labels and ideologies, and the power to assign these narratives and identities and to whom. In *S21*, stigmatising terms like 'trafficker' or 'criminal' are often not used in reference to powerful social elites involved in HT; rather, identifiers such as 'employer', 'marriage broker', or 'kiln owner' are used to designate these actors. If the purpose of *S21* is to stigmatise, expose, or denounce traffickers, one might expect that the usage of condemnatory terms such as 'criminal' or 'trafficker' in relation to these social elites is critical in constructing and communicating these narratives to public audiences. However, some actors featured in *S21* are called 'traffickers'. As will be shown in the next section, the assignment of the 'trafficker' label and the deviance that goes with it are largely dependent upon factors such as the ethnicity, age, nationality, class of those involved in trafficking, and the prevalent gender of the victims according to the type of HT represented.

REPRESENTATIONS OF 'TRAFFICKERS' IN *S21* NARRATIVES OF HT

The term 'trafficker' is used in *S21*, but inconsistently. In some episodes, the use of 'trafficker' and their presence are predominant. This is most evident in the episodes on the trafficking of women for sexual and/or domestic slavery, where 'traffickers' are referred to frequently by the presenter and programme makers, as for example in the online 'blurb' or text accompanying the episode 'Bridal Slaves':

> [online blurb:] Jamila, a former bride slave, says her **traffickers** kidnapped and drugged her, before selling her to an abusive man...
>
> Shafiq Khan, who runs a grassroots organisation dedicated to tracking down bride **traffickers** and their victims, explains: 'The girls do equal amounts of work in two jobs. They are sex slaves, not just to one man but a group of 10 or 12 men. Apart from that there is agriculture—working on the farms with animals from morning until night.'

In the 25-minute 'Bridal Slaves' episode, the word 'trafficker' is used in total eight times (including the two citations quoted above in the online blurb). In all but one instance, the term is used by the presenter in voiceovers and spoken in English:

> [presenter voiceover] For the past 20 years, bride traffickers have preyed on vulnerable young women from India's vast rural hinterland, promising to deliver them into a traditionally arranged marriage, but, in reality, selling them over and over into a life of sexual slavery and forced labour.

And in another presenter voiceover to describe a young male who is later identified as Shafiq Khan 'who runs a grassroots organisation dedicated to tracking down bride traffickers and the women who've fallen victim to their trade':

[presenter voiceover:] But there is a shortage of women in this region, sometimes as few as seven women for every ten men. It creates a ready market for bride traffickers.

Only once in 'Bridal Slaves' is the term used by someone else, by the aforementioned Shafiq Khan, in English subtitles:

We have come to this village before and talked to these people so we were a bit suspicious that he's a middle man and a trafficker.
[Omaar voiceover, walking through village walkways:] But with the men's denial of any involvement in trafficking, Shafiq will need to continue his search for harder evidence. He's now on the trail of a man whose contacts have identified as a marriage broker. Shafiq suspects he may be a bride trafficker.
[Omaar voiceover over scenes of a railway station:] Marriage may seem the best option for a woman who has been the victim of bride traffickers and transported thousands of miles from her home. But the real solution lies in India enforcing its own anti-slavery laws.

Traffickers are described by Omaar in another voiceover introducing a group of women brought together to discuss their experiences of being trafficked as

taken from their families against their will they claim by traffickers who use a mixture of false promises and violence. They were then simply sold into marriage, some of them many times over.

Presenter voiceover is heavily used across the episodes of *S21* to create the HT narratives. Victim testimonies also feature commonly throughout, but their usage of the term 'trafficker' to describe or label those who they identify as responsible for their trafficking is very different. It must be noted here that many of these victims speak in their own indigenous languages, which is not English. In all episodes of S21, including 'Bridal Slaves', the victims' voices are audible and their words are presented in translation into English in subtitles on the bottom of the screen. In these subtitles, the word 'trafficker' never appears. When the 'Bridal Slaves' women speak (in English subtitled translation) of those who have trafficked or abused them, they typically speak of 'the man' who 'bought', 'sold', 'forced', or 'beat' them. They do not use the word 'trafficker' to describe those who traffic them. What is more, they tend not to directly refer to a trafficker type agent at all, or only do so indirectly or obliquely, as for example in these typical quotations from the women describing their experiences:

> They injected me with drugs and beat me. Then I was sold on.
> I was sold to a man who had 8 girls and 4 boys. He took 6,000 Rupees ($123). After 15 days I was sold again for 10,000 Rupees ($205) to the man I'm with now.
> I would have to work all day in the heat then go home and get beaten. Is it worth living? ['Bridal Slaves']

What is also notable in these representations is how traffickers are spoken of in the passive or intransitive cases, as in first and second examples above. This is consistent with that Choi-Fitzpatrick's (2016, p. 10) previously quoted observation that in discourses of HT, traffickers lack 'object status'. They are portrayed above all as active agents who do as they like with relative impunity, but are not spoken of directly. The third example uses the intransitive case to describe what the woman does, which is to work all day and go home to get beaten by the man who has purchased her from the trafficker. These are examples of the diegetic narratives previously mentioned:

> I was brought here by a man to stay with his sister. Before the girls are brought here they're told they will see Delhi. When I was brought over they said I would be a wife.
> I was driven in a truck. After that I was sold to a blind man. Then I was sold to someone else and someone else after that. I was constantly being given drugs I said 'I don't want to go any further'. He said, 'Let's see how you don't want to go'. He would put my legs over the fire. ['Bridal Slaves']

Following the above testimony, the documentary cuts back to a previously featured tearful woman victim who is interviewed by Omaar, and whose words are presented in English translation subtitles:

> [unnamed woman:] I was sold for 5,000 Rupees.
> [Omaar:] 5,000 Rupees, that's about $120. So how did these men treat you?'
> [Woman:] They would hit and punch me. Day and night he would swear and beat me. I would have to work all day in the heat. My mind would be going round and round [makes circles in the air with her finger.] That's no

life. [Crying] What's the point? You go home and the man hits and beats you. Is it worth living? ['Bridal Slaves'].

The above segment is repeated twice in this episode. Throughout this episode, monetary amounts mentioned are translated by the presenter into US dollar currency, presumably so that western viewers can understand the commodification of people as an essential element of HT.

To briefly summarise, while 'trafficker' is used quite prominently in the episode on bridal slaves (the second most prominent usage of the seven episodes comprising *S21*), it is a term used almost exclusively by the presenter, and once (in subtitled translation) by a local male NGO worker. The women themselves are never quoted using it, though again their voices are audible and their words are presented in English translation subtitles. Rather, as cited above, they are quoted as using more ordinary words when referring to their traffickers as 'men', or alternatively concentrate solely on the abjection or disparity of their own condition, for example, in terms of the violent abuse they suffer at the hands of these men, the work they are forced to do, or the fact that they were falsely promised that they would be a 'wife'.

In contrast, in the episode entitled 'Charcoal Slaves', the term 'trafficker' is never used. This role is heavily implied, but the word itself is conspicuously absent. Like the women in the 'Bridal Slaves' episode which is located in rural India, the men in rural Brazil enslaved to make charcoal speak of those who traffic them in more indirect, oblique, and again passive/intransitive modes using ordinary language and focusing instead not on those who traffic them but their own suffering and plight:

[in English subtitles, headshot of the man, interspersed with family scenes]: We fell into it. Charcoal became really lucrative around here, you know. Here in Jacunda, unemployment is really a problem. We have to work to earn our day-to-day living and however little we get, it's all welcome. More than welcome.

The narrative focus here is on family, employment, the market for charcoal, and the need for work. There is no mention of criminals or criminality, men or traffickers.

A man is shown shovelling charcoal from a fire, with the presenter Omaar describing in voiceover how he was forced to breathe in the smoke-filled air. The victim speaks and his words appear in English translation subtitles along the bottom of the screen:

> We had no protective clothing, no masks, not even footwear, face guards or helmets. The place we lived in was a wooden shack. There was no electricity and no fridge. No oven, bathroom or even running water. It caused me lots of health problems. ['Charcoal Slaves']

Again, the focus is not on 'traffickers' but rather upon living conditions and the lack of proper safety equipment. There is no mention of those who are responsible for this, or should have provided better accommodation or protection. These agents are present only by implication, not explicitly made visible, audible, or otherwise named or known as responsible and accountable individuals. This failure to identify traffickers as criminal actors as a result of their elision of 'direct object status' as described by Choi-Fitzpatrick (2016) in narratives of HT could help explain the failures to deal with them via the legal-judicial framework with its concentration upon individual named criminals detailed at the beginning of this chapter. There are substantial divergences in terms of victim/ witness discourses and the law when it comes to identifying, discussing, and capturing (in the semiotics of language, visual iconography, and law) 'traffickers'.

The differences in narrative representations of traffickers even in a single documentary series are paramount. Consider the following example of ow another man describes his enslavement at the charcoal farm:

> Charcoal farming is the worst kind of work that exists as far as I am concerned. It's the most back-breaking. As you are out there in the jungle, right? People know what that's like, right? In the jungle, cutting away, getting scratched. I had malaria twice in a row. ['Charcoal Slaves']

But in response to this man, Omaar does not refer to 'traffickers' but rather 'employers':

> [Omaar]: And did the *employers* give you any assistance, whether it was because of getting malaria, or food, or someone else got sick, did you have any help from the employers in the work?' Man shakes his head 'No. Nothing. Just work. ['Charcoal Slaves', emphasis added]

Similar to 'Charcoal Slaves', the 'Food Chain Slaves' episode also deals exclusively with male victims. Two of the enslaved men interviewed speak of their traffickers thusly:

They watch.
  They tell you to eat...
  They are referred to by the men as 'security guards'. ['Food Chain Slaves']

As in the 'Charcoal Slaves' example, those responsible for trafficking the men in the 'Food Chain Slaves' are never described by their victims as 'traffickers'. The Soo brothers who are featured in this episode as traffickers who were brought to court to face slavery charges are visually represented in what appears to be amateur video footage walking silently from the court building in the manner of the famous Patterson-Giblin footage of 'Big Foot' (see Bader, Baker, & Mencken, 2011). This is a powerful visual semiotic that connotes a strong cultural narrative of strangeness, uniqueness, elusiveness, and cunning invention of those who traffic other human beings, rendering traffickers visually as mythical, alien, unknown, or even wild creatures who may or may not live among us. As Bader et al. (2011) explain, this constitutes a hyper masculine-oriented ideology of fearful yet desirable 'otherness' in which the uncertain and indeterminate identity of 'trafficker', like 'Big Foot', is semiotically represented and read by many audience members.

The reasons behind this usage of language and semiotics are open to debate, but a difference between these documentaries that immediately springs to mind is that the 'Bridal Slaves' episode is devoted entirely to female victims, whereas the 'Charcoal Slaves' and 'Food Chain Slaves' documentaries relate to victims who are all male. While the Indian women featured in 'Bridal Slaves' speak of those who traffic them as 'men' and not 'traffickers', the presenter uses the term 'trafficker' in this episode on this form of HT frequently. In contrast, the male victims featured in the 'Charcoal Slaves' (Brazil) and 'Food Chain Slaves' (Hawaii) rarely speak of those who traffic them, never use the term 'trafficker', and neither does the presenter. Instead, in 'Charcoal Slaves' and 'Food Chain Slaves' terms like 'employer' or 'security guards' are used to refer to those involved in or responsible for trafficking the men, aligning them and their activities to broader ideological and social discourses relating not to slavery, but to *work*. Narrative representations of this type of HT with predominantly male victims is formulated as a subcategory of business or enterprise, not HT.

Does this usage of 'trafficker' according to the prevailing gender of the victims extend to other episodes of *S21* and other types of HT? Let us return to the episode 'Sex Slaves' which deals exclusively with the trafficking of women in Europe. 'Trafficker' is used seven times in the episode 'Sex Slaves', most commonly by the presenter in voiceovers, but also by a local male lawyer named as Ian Visdova and a female NGO worker identified as Ana Revenco, who both work with female sex trafficking victims from Moldova:

> [Visdova in translation with subtitles]: A public employee earns a salary here of 100–150 Euros per month. That's why everybody wants? to go abroad and find a decent salary. *Traffickers* exploit the gap between life abroad and the poverty in Moldova.
>
> [Omaar voiceover:] The most common ploy used by Moldovan *traffickers* is to place a bogus job advert in the local newspaper *Maklak* [phonetic spelling]. La Strada's team monitors each edition. ['Sex Slaves']

Ana Revenco, Moldovan female anti-trafficking worker, speaking in English:

> The *traffickers* actually use violence, [unclear] it's psychology and emotions. From the very beginning until the very end. They play with that. They use their own fears or hopes to chain the person. ['Sex Slaves']

Undercover footage of traffickers is also presented in this episode. Images of two young local men dressed casually in t shirts and jeans and a recording of their voices translated in subtitles is featured:

> So how many girls do you want to see?
>
> [Omaar voiceover:] [The undercover reporter] was quickly introduced to sex *traffickers*.

This is a revealing excerpt, because while 'trafficker' is used by the presenter in the voiceover for this segment, in the recorded undercover video footage presented on screen, the names of the young men are accompanied by the word 'PIMP' in capitals across the bottom of the screen, for example, 'ALEX: PIMP'. The narrative representation of sex trafficking is thus a layered discursive construction, with the 'trafficker' identity built upon the foundational metanarrative of prostitution and its typical nomenclature. While the presenter describes these individuals as 'traffickers' in his voiceover, the visual subtext identities them as 'PIMPS', not 'criminals', or simply 'men'. What is more, as in this scene, these 'pimp/traffickers' are depicted as less powerful than other more socially elite 'businessmen/traffickers' featured in *S21*. A lawyer who prosecuted Alexandr 'Salun' Kovali, a 'trafficker' featured in 'Sex Slaves', explains how those who are prosecuted are typically poor, uneducated, low-level, local agents from an ethnic minority background:

> There are a lot of men like Salun who are free and live well here. Most of the time, only simple, low-level traffickers are convicted. ['Sex Slaves']

There are clearly different standards being applied to 'traffickers' in popular cultural genres and in law, and this is acknowledged in *S21*:

> [Omaar voiceover:] The fate of the two convicted sex traffickers highlights those double standards. Alexandr Kovali will spend the next 19 years locked in a Moldovan prison. Shaban Baran [another convicted trafficker] is back home in Turkey. And free. The Dutch government allowed him out of jail for one day, he absconded and never returned. Until the rich Western countries address the demand for prostitution, rather than profit from it, there will always be men like Kovali and Baran. And there will always be sex slaves behind these windows. ['Sex Slaves'].

While the word 'trafficker' and the figures of traffickers are presented in 'Sex Slavery' in the above passages, the language and visual semiotics in this episode tends to refer to these men and their activities in terms of the language typically used to define and discuss prostitution, for example, the sex 'trade', traffickers/users as 'pimps', 'clients' or 'buyers' of women who then 'sell them on'. At the same time, the language of 'business' is also utilised, as those involved are referred to as 'pimps' and 'traffickers', but also as 'recruiters' of women for 'work' in brothels or clubs.

In 'Sex Slaves' Omaar interviews the convicted trafficker Kovali in prison, who recalcitrantly uses the language of business to vehemently deny any involvement in HT. Ironically, he defends himself against charges of trafficking or prostitution by reference to the right to privacy of the 'girls' and their freedom to do as they choose outside of business hours:

> [Kovali:] The girls were paid as hostesses. What they did after 5am, after the club closed, is none of my business. It's their private life. [Kovali shrugs and uses body language that divests and distances him from involvement in prostitution or trafficking.] ['Sex Slaves']

As in the 'Charcoal Slaves' episode, this type of 'explanatory' discourse reflected in the various phenomenal narratives of HT constructed by and around those accused of trafficking involves the positioning and semiotics of traffickers as 'businessmen' and their alignment with ideologies of 'entrepreneurialism', 'work', 'recruitment', 'employment', 'supply and demand', and participation in the legitimate global market economy. In this respect, the framing of the problem of HT and traffickers is not strictly speaking in terms of illegal activity or individual criminality, but rather the opportunities offered to 'entrepreneurs' by the international 'market' in women by recent changes to the sex trade itself, or indeed by the trade in men in the charcoal factories for the automotive industry and its demand for pig iron. In these instances, such changes to global market economics and the legalisation of prostitution results in the increase in the trafficking of women from Eastern Europe, specifically Moldova, in response to the decriminalisation of prostitution in destination countries like Amsterdam and the relative economic deprivation in eastern European countries. These relate to the so called 'push and pull' factors cited in Chap. 1.

As Visdova explains, traffickers, poverty and economic migration go together:

[Visdova in English translation with subtitles]: A public employee earns a salary here of 100–150 Euros per month. That's why everybody wants to go abroad and find a decent salary. Traffickers exploit the gap between life abroad and the poverty in Moldova. ['Sex Slaves']

This quote and its role in the narrative representation of HT in the international sex trade is significant in that it reflects and invigorates broader public ambivalence toward perceptions and narratives of global economic migration (see Plambech, 2016).

CODA

In the 2016 documentary *Britain's Modern Slave Trade* (Al Jazeera, 2016, or *BMS*), the construction and usage of the term 'trafficker' and this identity are similar, but also different. In her testimony presented in English translation this time in a voiceover by a female translation, a female victim of sex trafficking refers to her traffickers as 'they' and 'the guys', similar to the women in 'Bridal Slaves':

'They brought thirty guys. Then they tied me to the bed and the guys did their job.' [sex trade]... [*BMST*]

Similarly, traffickers are later referred to by the presenter David Harrison as 'the man' who drops off food to a cannabis farm slave, and as 'pimps' in relation to sex traffickers, as in the 'Sex Slaves' episode of *S21*. The word 'trafficker' appears a number of times in the written text accompanying the *BMST* documentary on the Al Jazeera webpage in which the video is embedded. However, there is a distinct shift in the episode broadcast in the use of labels to identify sex traffickers as 'Romanian captors', 'an ex-boyfriend and his brother', and 'slave masters', and also to refer explicitly to women traffickers as a 'female ringleader', 'madam', and 'the bad lady'.

Other terms for traffickers in other types of HT relate to their activities as '[people] smugglers', 'Vietnamese gangs' or 'criminal gangs', 'drugs gang', each of these in relation to HT for cannabis farming. 'Smugglers' are further identified, in the forced labour trade, as family members, as for example in the example presented of a nail bar in East London, in which the salon owner has 'smuggled' his sister into the UK to work illegally. In an interview in *BMS*, Kevin Hyland, UK Anti-Slavery Commissioner, refers not to legitimate or illegitimate actors or 'traffickers', but rather to the disappearance of these roles in the often-unwitting blurring of 'The legitimate and the illegitimate economies [that have] become one in some ways ... because companies and people don't realise ... they are ... using modern day slaves in their supply chain'. In contrast, the Salvation Army worker who is featured in *BMS* consistently and explicitly uses the term 'traffickers' to refer to those involved in HT.

CONCLUSION

This chapter presents a selection of representations of 'traffickers' as presented in the seven 25-minute long episodes of the Al Jazeera produced documentary series *Slavery: A Twenty-first Century Evil* (2011), and the 47-minute long documentary *Britain's Modern Slave Trade* (2016), and an analysis of them from a cultural criminological perspective. This analysis reveals multiple aspects of this complex and multi-dimensional roles and the emplotment of traffickers within popular narratives of HT/modern slavery. In accordance with traditional theodicy conceptualisations of, in Leibniz's famous phrase, the 'problem of evil' (Dearey, 2014; Ricoeur & Pelauer, 1985), the focus is primarily on named individuals who are presented as subject to accusation, conviction, and censure, whether in criminal court or less formal social settings. What these narrative representations of traffickers reveal is the fragility and failure of western criminal justice systems to (a) recognise and (b) deal effectively with traffickers, even on the rare occasions when they do face criminal charges. *S21* portrays these traffickers within narratives of injustice, crimes are not being prevented or dealt with effectively by state(s), and criminals are not being reformed. Even in instances when individual traffickers are accused, convicted, and jailed, they still consistently, and often vehemently, deny any wrongdoing. The semiotics of their identity narratives suggest a potent mixture of mystery, repulsion, fear, and desire, reminiscent of the 'white slavery' mythos cited by de Villiers (2016) and Namias (1992). Victims, as featured in these documentaries, do not identify or speak of them in ways that are amenable with modern criminal justice systems.

In its various usages, the term 'trafficker' is not clearly defined nor is its meaning or application consistent across the different episodes of *S21*. The most decisive factor influencing the usage of the term 'trafficker' is by the *gender of victims*; types of HT that involve only or primarily women and the sex trade tend to feature the word 'trafficker' in the documentary narratives. Whereas forms of HT involving men as victims for non-sexual purposes tend to eschew the label 'trafficker' in favour of terminology relating to business and enterprise to refer to these actors, for example, factory or kiln 'owners', 'security guards', 'employers', 'businessmen', 'barons', 'exporters', and the like. What is more, the lower status, local and ethnic minority men involved in the trafficking of women for sex are also identified as 'pimps' as well as 'traffickers', doubly stigmatising them as the result of their intimate involvement with the women they traffic and their own ethnicities, nationalities, relatively low socio-economic statuses, and masculinities. However, the language of 'business' can also be applied to these actors too, for example, in their role as 'recruiters' as well as 'pimps'. With respect to these lower-level male traffickers, the label of 'victim' or the recognition that these men (and women) can sometimes be victims too is not applied in either *S21* or *BMST*.

The voice of who is speaking, and how, is also significant. There is a liberal use of presenter voiceover throughout the episodes of *S21*, and it is within these that the term 'trafficker' most often appears. When victims of HT are interviewed in *S21*, their testimonies are often presented in English translation and in subtitles. This is somewhat different in the later Al Jazeera documentary *Britain's Modern Slave Trade* (2016). The women victims featured in *S21* do not use term 'trafficker' when discussing those who traffic them, tending to focus more upon their own experiences of what they have suffered at the hands of the 'men' who have abused and/or exploited them, if they directly refer to these individuals at all. In contrast, the presenter of *BMST* tends to use language relating to forms of transnational organised crime such as 'smuggling' or national or 'gang' related criminality, or terms more reflective of the relationship between the victim and the perpetrator. The term 'trafficker' is eschewed by the presenter of BMST but is consistently and explicitly used in this documentary by a British NGO worker from the Salvation Army who works with HT victims.

Throughout *S21*, even where less powerful men are involved in HT, if their victims are male, they are still less likely to be labelled 'traffickers' than those involved in trafficking women for the sex trade. The presence of males in the victim population is significant in the identification and usage of the word 'trafficker'. In instances where both males and females are trafficked—for example, child slavery, prison slavery, bonded slavery—in *S21*, those who traffic them are never referred to as either 'traffickers' or 'criminals' by the presenter, NGO workers, victims or the traffickers themselves. If it is women only who are trafficked, and if they are trafficked for work in the sex industry, then the word 'trafficker' is used, but almost always by the presenter, never by the victims themselves.

This indicates the primary significance of victims' gender and potency of prostitution metanarratives, and to a lesser extent the ethnicities and social status of HT offenders in the formulation and construction of the narratives and identities of 'traffickers' in popular criminology or 'true crime' discourses. This presents substantial challenges to the necessity or desirability of a special term 'trafficker' as cited in the Palermo Protocol to identify and/or stigmatise these individuals. The appearance and usage of such 'new' linguistic terms could have the effect of generating a sense of 'insider' knowledge on the part of audiences, with very little to substantiate the clarity or stability of the words, or their equitable use as stigmatising labels and/or legal terms. By presenting audiences with a new word to use to understand HT (that is, 'trafficker'), such true crime documentary programmes makers may be conveying a false sense of understanding and knowledge of the realities of HT to viewers, by over-emphasising the exceptionalism, homogeneity, power, cunning, or strangeness of those who traffic human beings by giving them a new label of their own.

One of the most notable elements of the use of 'trafficker' in *S21* is that it is, with one exception, used only by the presenter, almost exclusively in voiceover. Presenter voiceover is heavily used throughout *S21* to construct the documentary narratives of differing types of HT in *S21*. As a feminist cultural criminologist, I am struck by the fact that none of the women featured in *S21* used this term to describe or identify those who trafficked them. That they referred to 'men' or sometimes even 'husbands', or no one in particular at all, is in many ways more revealing of the realities and lived experiences of HT and human traffickers in their everyday lives. These testimonies are framed by the daily experiences of women (and men) around the world for whom the trauma of (sexual) violence and exploitation is still very much the norm. It does not require a special word, or role, raising the question of why such a term is introduced, who and in what positions the men who use it are doing so, and why. Questions are also raised about what such a term conveys to audiences who purport to understand HT or victims or HT, to enable them to recognise or identify a 'trafficker', as opposed to a criminal, conman, fraudster, kidnapper, or rapist; or indeed a brother, husband, pimp, 'bad lady', businessman, or just a man.

REFERENCES

Al Jazeera. (2011). *Modern Slavery: A Twenty-first Century Evil.* Television series. Presented by Rageh Omaar. Retrieved October 19, 2017, from http://www.aljazeera.com/programmes/slaverya21stcenturyevil/

Al Jazeera. (2016). *Britain's Modern Slave Trade: Al Jazeera Investigates.* Television series. Presented by David Harrison. Retrieved October 19, 2017, from https://interactive.aljazeera.com/aje/2016/uk-slavery-sex-slave-smuggling-investigation/index.html

Bader, C. D., Baker, J. O., & Mencken, F. C. (2011). *Paranormal America* (2nd ed.). New York: NYU Press.

Choi-Fitzpatrick, A. (2016). The good, the bad, the ugly: Human rights violators in comparative perspective. *Journal of Human Trafficking, 2*(1), 1–14.

Cohen, S. (2001). *States of denial: Knowing about atrocities and suffering.* Cambridge: Polity Press.

Dearey, M. (2014). *Making sense of evil: An interdisciplinary approach.* London: Palgrave Macmillan.

De Villiers, N. (2016). Rebooting trafficking. *Anti-Trafficking Review,* (7), 161–181.

Dussich, J. P. J. (undated). Victimology—Past, present and future. *131st International Senior Seminar Visiting Experts' Papers Series.* Retrieved October 19, 2017, from http://www.unafei.or.jp/english/pdf/RS_No70/No70_12VE_Dussich.pdf

Edwards, A., & Gill, P. (Eds.). (2003). *Transnational organised crime: Perspectives on global security.* London: Routledge.

Engdahl, H. (2002). *Witness literature: Proceedings of the Nobel centennial symposium.* Singapore: World Scientific Publishers.

Gotch, K. (2016). Preliminary data on a sample of perpetrators of domestic trafficking for sexual exploitation: Suggestions for research and practice. *Journal of Human Trafficking, 2*(1), 99–109.

Leishman, F., & Mason, P. (2004). *Policing and the media: Facts, fictions and factions.* Cullompton: Willan Press.

Lemert, E. (1967). *Human deviance, social problems and social control.* Englewood Cliffs, NJ: Prentice-Hall.

Lifetime Television. (2005 to present). *Human Trafficking.* Television series. Produced by Lifetime Television.

Linebaugh, P. (2006). *The London hanged: Crime and civil society in the eighteenth century* (2nd ed.). London: Verso.

Namias, J. (1992). *White captives: Gender and ethnicity on the American Frontier.* Chapel Hill and London: University of North Carolina Press.

Plambech, S. (2016, September). The art of the possible: Making films on sex work migration and human trafficking. *Anti-Trafficking Review, 7*, 182–199.

Rawlings, P. (1998). True crime. *The British criminology conferences: Selected proceedings. Volume 1: Emerging themes in criminology.* Papers from the British Criminology Conference, Loughborough University, 18–21 July 1995. Published September 1998. Editors: Jon Vagg and Tim Newburn. Retrieved October 19, 2017, from http://www.britsoccrim.org/volume1/010.pdf

Ricoeur, P., & Pelauer, D. (1985, December). Evil: A challenge to philosophy and theology. *Journal of the American Academy of Religion, 53*(4), 75th Anniversary Meeting of the American Academy of Religion, pp. 635–648.

Shen, A. (2016). Female perpetrators in internal child trafficking in China: An empirical study. *Journal of Human Trafficking, 2*(1), 63–77.

The Economist. (2017, July 1). Why is Al Jazeera under threat. *The Economist.* Retrieved November 8, 2017, from https://www.economist.com/news/middle-east-and-africa/21724366-arab-worlds-leading-news-channel-independent-voice-or-propaganda

The Wire. (2002–2008). Television series. HBO. Creator: David Simons.

Conclusion

In this book, we explored portrayals of transnational human trafficking (THT) presented by various media, and investigated the relationship between these depictions and the realities of trafficking. We linked our findings to existing research literature as well as taking account of the experiences of law enforcement, NGOs, and media practitioners. Our methods were drawn from various critical fields and theoretical areas. The strength of such a multi-methodological approach is that consistently reoccurring representations can, with a great level of confidence, be said to form part, if not the core, of the current master narrative of trafficking.

Our analyses show that throughout newspaper articles, there is a pre-occupation with female victims of sex trafficking. This pre-occupation sustains a view of trafficking in which only young, female, compliant, silent, agentless subjects of sex trafficking are actually considered victims. As a result, only these victims are likely to receive judicial remedy and/or substantial formal post-trafficking support. Less 'ideal' but nonetheless real victims, often male, are at best invisible, or are stigmatised and criminalised, often held responsible for their own victimisation. These gender stereotypes are perpetuated in crime fiction, which often portrays traffickers as male and violent, whereas female accomplices play a supporting role. However, the analysis of British and Scandinavian crime novels suggests that fiction does allow for greater nuance, particularly in its portrayal of

© The Author(s) 2018
C. Gregoriou (ed.), *Representations of Transnational Human Trafficking*, https://doi.org/10.1007/978-3-319-78214-0

child trafficking victims. We argue that crime fiction promotes a greater understanding of the different forms of exploitation to which trafficked children are subjected. These include child soldiering, domestic slavery, and organ trafficking, as well as sexual exploitation.

In the Al Jazeera documentaries, the identity of perpetrators is linked to the gender of their victims, in the sense that those who traffic women for sexual purposes are identified as traffickers, whereas those who traffic men for non-sexual exploitation are identified, predominantly, as businessmen. This again suggests that sex-trafficked women tend to be recognised as victims of trafficking, whereas trafficked men tend not to be. The language and discourses of witness, testimony, and prevailing cultural paradigms of 'normal' daily life and family practices often raised questions about the construction of programmer or other expert narrative explanations.

Across text types, we find a focus on official responses to trafficking, especially heroic rescues, to the exclusion of critical and alternative options. In British newspapers, trafficking is consistently presented as a foreign, imported problem, which, as our literature review also indicates, allows the British state to portray itself as heroically responding to threats to its national security and those deemed worthy of protection. However, certain British newspapers criticise the criminal justice response to the supposedly foreign threat of traffickers. The analysis of British and Scandinavian crime fiction indicates a recurring theme of family 'allowing' their children to be trafficked, suggesting also that states take on a paternalistic, almost patronising parental role in lieu of the actual family. On the other hand, the Al Jazeera documentaries, as well as various newspaper articles, show that the criminal justice responses fall short. Our analysis of Serbian newspapers also demonstrates that these stories are manipulated to fit the news agenda. These findings indicate that the prevalent representation of trafficking is, as also suggested by media practitioners attending our symposium, 'shaped' by the economic necessity of 'selling' a story to the readership. Our literature review also demonstrates that responses to victims are severely lacking and seem to serve more to make state actors 'look good' than actually help those affected by trafficking. This focus on official responses, however, glosses over the role of Britain and other Western states in sustaining the global inequalities that contribute to the problem.

Our analyses suggest that representations of HT are often simplistic, focusing on heroic responses. These representations may be, as per our Introduction, complicit in the perpetuation of global inequality. As such, alternative perspectives must be presented and shared, and structural factors must be focused on (Gregoriou, 2017). These measures are crucial for general public awareness of the complex realities of labour- and sexual exploitation.

REFERENCE

Gregoriou, C. (2017). *PaCCS policy brief: The representation of transnational human trafficking in present-day news media, true crime and fiction.* [Online]. Leeds: PaCCS. Retrieved February 13, 2018, from http://www.paccsresearch.org.uk/policy-briefings/transnational-human-trafficking/

INDEX[1]

[1] Note: Page numbers followed by 'n' refer to notes.

© The Author(s) 2018
C. Gregoriou (ed.), *Representations of Transnational Human
Trafficking*, https://doi.org/10.1007/978-3-319-78214-0

O

Offender, 7, 8, 12, 30, 33, 52n21, 122, 125, 140

Omaar, Rageh, 121, 126–128, 130–133, 135, 136

Other, otherness, 2, 3, 5, 6, 9, 11, 13, 14, 16–18, 29, 31, 37, 39, 40, 44, 46, 47, 49–51, 52n21, 53–55, 63, 67n9, 70–72, 75–82, 91–93, 95, 96n8, 98, 99n10, 102–107, 118, 119, 121, 122, 122n2, 124–126, 128, 134–136, 138, 144

P

Paedophile, 46, 69, 70, 97

Palermo Protocol, 2, 4, 5, 26, 30, 90, 91, 91n2, 120, 140

People, The, 65, 75

Perpetrator, 31, 36, 46–47, 49, 52, 53, 55, 74, 75, 78, 93, 96, 109, 118, 122, 125, 140, 144
    'perp', 124

Photographs, 11, 34, 53, 127

Photojournalism, 54

Police, v, vi, 12, 16, 37, 39, 42, 49, 50, 52, 52n21, 65, 66, 71, 72, 75, 79, 95, 97, 99, 104, 104n20, 105, 109, 124, 126

Policy, vi, 3, 7, 9, 45, 50, 51, 72, 81, 82, 118, 118n1, 119, 121
    makers, 3, 7, 45, 118, 118n1

Political dissent, 124, 127

Politika, 64n4, 66–69, 72, 73, 78

Pop culture, 3, 7, 45

Pornography, 42, 71, 92

Poverty, 5, 8, 14, 15, 17, 39, 72, 80, 82, 92, 96, 135, 137

Power
    economic, 16
    material, 13
    social, 51, 128

soft, 13

Pravda, 64n4, 67

Pregled, 64n4, 66

Press, vi, 26, 27, 40, 52n21, 64n4, 65, 66, 69–72, 75–77, 79, 118
    See also News

Propp, Vladimir, 93, 93n4

Prosecution, 12, 14, 79, 110

Prostitution, 16, 27, 39, 42, 47, 48, 65, 68, 73, 76, 77, 79, 81, 92, 99, 106, 135–137, 140
    See also Sex, work

Public, 3–5, 7, 9, 18, 19, 27, 45, 62, 63, 66–68, 70, 74–76, 79–83, 90, 93n3, 95, 97, 99, 105, 109, 110, 118, 118n1, 119, 121, 124, 128, 135, 137, 145
    sphere, 118, 119, 121, 124

Punishment, 74–76, 107, 121, 127, 128

Q

Qatar, 120

R

RACE Project, 2, 4

Refugee, 2, 18, 27, 30, 44, 50, 53, 54, 71, 91, 103

Reporting, vi, 2, 4, 8, 13, 18, 29, 31, 36, 41, 47, 51–53
    See also News

Representation, v, 2–19, 26–55, 62, 74–76, 90–97, 96n7, 99, 100n11, 101n14, 102, 103, 107–111, 118–126, 129–138, 143, 144

Right-wing, 16

Romani/Roma, 46, 65, 70, 95, 96, 101n15

RQTR, 27n4

Russia, 74

GPSR Compliance
The European Union's (EU) General Product Safety Regulation (GPSR) is a set
of rules that requires consumer products to be safe and our obligations to
ensure this.

If you have any concerns about our products, you can contact us on

ProductSafety@springernature.com

In case Publisher is established outside the EU, the EU authorized
representative is:

Springer Nature Customer Service Center GmbH
Europaplatz 3
69115 Heidelberg, Germany